Scripted

Four One Act Plays

By

Bob Stone

©Bob Stone 2023

All rights reserved

No part of this publication may be reproduced, stored in a retrieval system, or transmitted in any form or by any means, without the prior permission of the author, nor be otherwise circulated without the author's prior consent in any form or binding other than that in which it is published.

The moral right of the author has been asserted.

Please see notes for performance rights.

CONTENTS

Introduction..5

In After School..7

Crossing the Border...55

Some of Us Are Looking At the Stars..103

Night of the Long Beards......................................145

Afterword..207

Dedicated to all members of Lucilla D.S, past and present, especially the late, great David Sumner, the perfect Alastair Palmer, and Wendy Stone, for whom the roles of Lisa Irving, The Young Woman and Alicia Winters were created

Introduction

Years ago, in fact, what seems now like a lifetime ago, I was a member of an amateur dramatic society. It is called the Lucilla Dramatic Society and is based in Crosby, near Liverpool. Look them up; they're very good. I was a member for some twenty years until circumstances meant that I could no longer give the commitment that I had previously given, so I left. I don't regret my time with the Lucilla at all; I met my wife there, if nothing else, which is obviously a good thing.

I joined the Lucilla because I had done a bit of acting at school and enjoyed it. The camaraderie of being involved in a show is a wonderful thing, and I was delighted to find it again. There was a distinct lack of young men in the society at that time, and although I wasn't *that* young and didn't really have the build or the looks to be leading man material, I got some decent parts (more by default than anything else), including – and you'd never think it to look at me now – the Cary Grant part in *Arsenic and Old Lace*. After a while, it became apparent to me (and I'm sure to everyone else) that I wasn't actually all that good, so I took up directing instead. In common with many amateur groups, the Lucilla had limited resources and a limited number of members, so sometimes choosing a play was difficult. However, I had a go at remedying that problem by writing my own. I knew the stage we would be performing on and what scenery and props were available. More importantly, I knew the age range of actors I could call on. This meant I could tailor the scripts accordingly and write plays I knew I could cast and set. And so it began.

Over the following years, I wrote and directed a number of one-act plays. Some were more serious, some were comedies, some were specifically written for the annual Christmas party (including *Night of the Long Beards*, which you can read in this volume). Most of the plays went down well, and some went down very well indeed. The Lucilla have, for example, performed *In After School* three times, and one of those productions was after I had left, so I thoroughly enjoyed coming back as a guest to see it. The plays were mostly written on a word processor I had at the time and stored on floppy disc (remember them?) I managed to transfer some of them onto more modern storage systems, but most remain on the floppies and I'm not even sure if I have the discs now. We've moved house since then and got rid of a lot of stuff we didn't think we'd need anymore. Luckily, the plays I have reproduced in this volume are some of which I am most proud. I hope they don't appear too dated now; there are some notes on that in the afterword. There are also some notes on production rights if anyone should happen to want to perform any of them. In any case, I hope you enjoy reading them as much as I enjoyed writing and performing them.

Bob Stone

July 2023

In After School

A One Act Drama

CAST IN ORDER OF APPEARANCE

ALASTAIR PALMER
STEPHEN BELLINGHAM
PHIL TRAVIS
LISA IRVING
CHRISTINE STEIN

The action takes place in the English room of a comprehensive school.

The time is early 2000s.

A room at a comprehensive school. As we later learn, this room is a building in its own right, separate from the rest of the school. There are desks and chairs as befit a small classroom and shelves with books here and there. The wall r. has a black (or white) board. There is one window in the back wall and a windowless door up l..

As the play opens, ALASTAIR PALMER is seated at one of the desks with a pile of papers in front of him. PALMER is a rather morose man in his late fifties and is writing remarks on one of the papers. When he has finished, he slaps the pen down, sighs and runs his fingers through his hair.

The door opens and STEPHEN BELLINGHAM, a good-natured man in his early fifties, enters.

BELLINGHAM

Surely it can't be that bad, Alastair? Anyway, one last push and we can all go home for the weekend.

PALMER

It hasn't been bad, Stephen. Not as such. I'm just catching up with some marking.

BELLINGHAM

Couldn't you do it over Easter?

PALMER

I'm not taking the sixth forms' essays on *Titus Andronicus* to Tenerife. Dora would never forgive me.

BELLINGHAM

How is Dora?

PALMER

Fine.

BELLINGHAM

I expect she's looking forward to the holiday.

PALMER

(*rather sharply*) Stephen, Dora is fine, all right?

BELLINGHAM

I only asked.

PALMER

I could have done with today to pack. These training days are a pain in the backside.

BELLINGHAM

Got to be done, though. We'd only have been teaching otherwise.

PALMER

A small consolation. And why Stein elected to hold ours in this Godforsaken shack, I'll never understand.

BELLINGHAM

(*adopting a mock-pompous manner*) Isolation focuses the mind, my dear Alastair.

PALMER

Yes, well, there's a word for that. But couldn't we be isolated somewhere else? I mean, this place was probably an air-raid shelter in the war. They probably used to put naughty kids here in solitary confinement.

BELLINGHAM

But it is the English room. You notice, though, that the computer labs are right in the middle of the school and not in the back of beyond.

(The door opens and LISA IRVING, an attractive young teacher in her twenties, and PHIL TRAVIS, who is not that much older, enter. They are laughing at some shared joke.)

TRAVIS

Oh. Isn't she back yet?

PALMER

I thought she went to the staff room with you.

LISA

We didn't go up.

(She nods towards TRAVIS and mimes smoking.)

BELLINGHAM

Oh, I see.

TRAVIS

(*to PALMER*) Cheer up, Alastair. This time tomorrow, you'll be on your way to sunnier climes.

BELLINGHAM

Yes, but in the meantime, he's got to plough through the sixth form's assassination of Tightarse Andronicus.

LISA

Are they terrible?

PALMER

Not *terrible*. Just...well...disappointing. They sit in class all attention and questions and go home and write like they've never read the play before.

TRAVIS

I get quite nostalgic for the days when teaching the sixth was a welcome respite from the rest of the school.

PALMER

You haven't been here long enough to remember that.

LISA

Come on, Phil. Some of the sixth-formers are still like that.

TRAVIS

Name any three.

LISA

Well... there's Gillian Wesley. She's very nice and really helpful. And Matthew Hudd. And what about Julie Winters?

PALMER

Hudd? Do you teach him?

LISA

I did last year.

PALMER

Hudd is someone I really don't like.

TRAVIS

Which one's he? Is he one of those reptiles who hang around the gym selling crack to the first years?

LISA

Do they do that? I'm sure Matthew doesn't.

BELLINGHAM

None of them do. They smoke, of course, but Phil thinks if he says that, we'll have a go at him.

PALMER

Hudd doesn't smoke, either. He's actually very civilised. I just don't like him. He doesn't look at you; have you noticed that? He looks like he knows something you don't. Actually, he reminds me of a cat.

LISA

I never had any problems with him. Anyway, his GCSE results must tell you something.

TRAVIS

He probably fancies you.

LISA

Phil!

PALMER

I don't doubt his results. He's highly intelligent. I think that's partly what's so unsettling. Maybe it's just me, but I find him insolent. I had to put him in detention for it last week.

BELLINGHAM

What for? Cheek? That's a bit strong.

PALMER

It wasn't just cheek. It's the way he looks at you as though you can't teach him anything he doesn't know. He flatly refused to do an exercise I'd set. Said he didn't see the point.

BELLINGHAM

All the same....

(The door opens, and CHRISTINE STEIN, the Head of Department, enters. She is in her late forties and takes a no-nonsense approach. She breezes in, leaving the door open.)

MRS. STEIN

Oh. You're all here.

BELLINGHAM

Just waiting for you.

MRS. STEIN

Well, I'm here now. Now come on, let's get started. That way, we might just be finished by four. Shut the door, Lisa, or we'll all freeze to death.

(LISA does so as everyone else sits down. Then she joins them, sitting next to TRAVIS.)

MRS. STEIN

Now then. I think we've got the curriculum sorted out, and I wanted to spend a bit of time discussing extra-curricular activities. Stephen, you've prepared a few ideas.

BELLINGHAM

(digging in his bag) Yes. The school plays are all very well, but I'd like to see a bit more in the way of drama for its own sake. I've got here... Oh hell. I must have left it in the staff-room.

MRS. STEIN

What have you lost?

BELLINGHAM

I've been making a few enquiries round other schools and I've made notes...

MRS. STEIN

Do you need the notes?

BELLINGHAM

It would be a help. I won't be a minute.

MRS. STEIN

Go on, then.

LISA

Stephen, could you do me a favour and pick up my mobile while you're there? I left it charging by the fridge.

BELLINGHAM

(*with a sigh*) Anyone else want anything while I'm there?

(*As no-one replies, he gets up and goes to the door. It will not open.*)

BELLINGHAM

Lisa, is this supposed to be a joke?

LISA

What?

BELLINGHAM

The door's locked.

TRAVIS

(*going over to help him*) It's probably just jammed with the damp weather. (*He tries the door*) You're right; it is. Lisa?

LISA

(*indignant*) Well, I didn't lock it.

BELLINGHAM

You were the last one near the damn thing.

LISA

I didn't lock it, I tell you. What do you think I am?

TRAVIS

(*crouching to peer through the key-hole*) No, hang on. The key's in the lock outside.

PALMER

Someone's trying to be funny. Probably that David Fielding.

BELLINGHAM

Don't be silly, Alastair. There's no one in the maths department with a sense of humour. Anyway, Dave said they'd be finishing early.

TRAVIS

Well, someone's done it. (*He hammers on the door and shouts*) Hey! Open the door! (*Pause*) Come on! A joke's a joke.

LISA

(going over to the window) I can't see anyone out there.

MRS. STEIN

I'll have someone's head for this.

BELLINGHAM

(who has picked something up from the floor) What's this? Looks like a note.

LISA

What does it say?

BELLINGHAM

(reading) "You're all in detention."

PALMER

I don't believe it. It's one of the kids.

MRS. STEIN

Do you recognise the writing, Stephen?

BELLINGHAM

No. I don't think so. It doesn't look like one of the younger kids' writing. Sixth-former, maybe. Don't recognise...no...wait. Alastair, you've got some essays there.

PALMER

It's not likely to be a sixth-former, is it?

BELLINGHAM

I'm not sure. Let's see.

(BELLINGHAM goes over to PALMER and starts looking through the essays he has in front of him.)

BELLINGHAM

(taking an essay) Isn't that it? Simon Reece.

PALMER

Wouldn't surprise me. He's always trying to wind me up. Only the other day....

BELLINGHAM

No, look, the 'e's are different. *(Looks through some more)* No... No... It looks more like male handwriting... no... There it is. Matthew Hudd.

MRS. STEIN

Matthew Hudd? It doesn't seem like him.

LISA

Alastair was only saying before that he doesn't like him.

MRS. STEIN

I'm not very fond of him myself at the moment if it's him. Why would he do a thing like this?

TRAVIS

Alastair only went and put him in detention.

PALMER

So, it's revenge. That's typical.

MRS.STEIN

All the same....

BELLINGHAM

Hang on... there's something else... the other side of the note. *(He turns the note over)* The cheeky....

MRS. STEIN

What does it say?

BELLINGHAM

I don't think you want me to read it out.

MRS. STEIN

Oh, for Heaven's sake, read it!

BELLINGHAM

"Ask Mrs. Stein where her husband is."

Blackout

INTERLUDE

For this and all subsequent interludes, the lights fade down on the rest of the stage while a spot comes up on the subject of the interlude. The rest of the cast remain frozen in the background. In this case, the subject is MRS.STEIN. The spot in this interlude should ideally have a blue colour to suggest the light given off by a TV screen. MRS. STEIN is no longer in the school but sitting at home with an imaginary remote control, watching television.

MRS. STEIN

EastEnders is a gloomy programme. At least Coronation Street has a bit of humour, even though it often doesn't seem very real. In EastEnders, people are always having affairs and getting divorced or dying. Sometimes I wish he had died. At least then, I could have put him in the ground and got on with things. Now I've got to carry on knowing he's walking around with a younger model. A quiz show. I never knew that there was so much garbage on television. But then, I never watched it much. There always seemed so much more to do. Marking. Preparing. Paperwork. God, I hate paperwork. I know the rest of the staff laugh about it, saying I thrive on it, but there's so much to do. They're always moving the goalposts with their targets and key stages and league tables. I've got to keep up. If I don't, who will? It's not my fault. He never complained about the money, just about me being too busy or too tired. Yes, I get tired. Everyone gets tired these days. He didn't have to leave me for it. Just let him wait. One day she'll get older. She'll get tired and lined and grey and start to sag. Maybe he'll leave her then, too. But he didn't have to leave ME!

She breaks down.

Blackout

(When the lights come back up, MRS. STEIN has composed herself and it is as if the interlude had never happened.)

MRS. STEIN

Well? Aren't you going to ask me then?

PALMER

It's none of our business.

MRS. STEIN

It was bound to come out: sooner or later. Though how Matthew Hudd found out beats me. My husband has left me.

(Pause.)

LISA

I'm sorry. We had no idea. Honestly.

MRS. STEIN

I didn't want anyone to have any idea, Lisa. That was the point. It wasn't your concern.

BELLINGHAM

When did it happen?

MRS.STEIN

(fighting to keep control) Six weeks ago.

LISA

Six weeks!

MRS. STEIN

I came home after school one day, and he'd gone. Just like that. *(Pause)* Well, this is all very well, but it doesn't solve our current problem. We're still locked in.

LISA

I'll just ring the staff room on my mobile...

BELLINGHAM

I thought you said it was in the staff room.

LISA

Oh.

TRAVIS

Oh great. It's no good to us there, is it?

LISA

Where's yours, then?

TRAVIS

(checking his pockets) Er...at home. Christine?

MRS. STEIN

In my bag. *(Pause)* In the staff room. Oh, I don't believe this! It's the twenty-first century and no-one's got a mobile? It's all we can do to get the kids off them. Has no one even got one you've confiscated?

(BELLINGHAM and PALMER just shrug.)

MRS. STEIN

We'll have to find another answer, then.

TRAVIS

What about the window?

MRS. STEIN

What about it?

TRAVIS

Someone could climb out. Lisa, maybe.

LISA

Me?

TRAVIS

You're the slimmest.

PALMER

Have you ever tried opening the window in here? It was painted shut last time the building was decorated. It's stifling in here in the summer.

BELLINGHAM

That must have been, what, six or seven years ago?' I'll be jammed solid.

LISA

There must be some other way out.

PALMER

Well, if you can think of one, my dear, you're welcome to try it.

LISA

There's no need to be nasty. I only said.

MRS. STEIN

I suggest we all try and calm down and think. We're supposed to be intelligent people.

TRAVIS

We could break the door down.

MRS. STEIN

And damage school property? I don't think so.

BELLINGHAM

It *is* an emergency.

MRS. STEIN

I doubt the Headmaster would see it like that.

BELLINGHAM

Maybe the Headmaster would prefer us to stay in here over Easter.

MRS. STEIN

Not until we've exhausted any other options.

LISA

I saw a film once where they pushed a piece of paper under the door, knocked the key onto the paper and pulled it back through.

(Pause)

PALMER

Ladies and gentlemen, the benefits of media studies. It doesn't really work, you know. How many doors have got that much of a gap at the bottom?

TRAVIS

It's worth a go. *(He picks up a piece of paper and goes over to the door. He crouches beside it, looking through the keyhole)* The key's gone!

PALMER

Looks like young Hudd watches the same films as our Ms. Irving here.

BELLINGHAM

Yes, but it also means he's still around. Lisa, can you see him?

(LISA goes to the window and looks out.)

LISA

I can't see anyone.

TRAVIS

Then he must be out there. *(Goes to the door and bangs on it)* Hudd! Matthew! Open this door at once! *(Pause)* Matthew!

MRS. STEIN

Either he's deaf or ignoring you.

TRAVIS

(Banging harder on the door) He'd better not be. MATTHEW!

MRS. STEIN

Come away, Phil. I don't think that's the answer.

TRAVIS

(Moving away) Well, I hope Hudd has some decent answers when we get out of here because he's going to need them.

PALMER

Or what? Are you going to keep him in detention? Isn't that what started this? Maybe you could give him some lines, write a hundred times, "I won't keep my teachers locked in a classroom." Or what about giving him a good slapping? What do you suggest we do with him, Psycho?

LISA

Psycho?

PALMER

Didn't you know? That's what the kids call him. And I think he rather likes being known as the hard man.

TRAVIS

Don't be ridiculous.

LISA

I never knew they called you that. It doesn't sound like you, Phil.

PALMER

How would you know?

LISA

(embarrassed but defiant) I've worked with him for nearly two years.

PALMER

I've known him for three. And I've seen people like him before. People who relish keeping discipline.

TRAVIS

At least I get discipline. Your classroom sounds like a bloody riot's going on.

PALMER

And Matthew Hudd really respects you, doesn't he?

MRS. STEIN

This is all very interesting but not very constructive. We're still locked in and arguing won't help.

BELLINGHAM

Shush a minute. I thought I heard something.

(Pause)

BELLINGHAM

Maybe not.

PALMER

(Going over to the door) No, Stephen, you did. It's another note.

BELLINGHAM

Another one?

PALMER

(chuckling to himself) I rather like this one. "What do Mr. Travis and Miss Irving get up to behind the bike sheds?"

Blackout

INTERLUDE

When the spot comes up, LISA and TRAVIS are sitting next to each other. She has her head on his shoulder.

LISA

I can't help it. I just like the way he makes me feel. He makes me feel special, and no one did that before. But that's what you get when you're the youngest of three, all girls. It didn't matter what I did. Mum and Dad just never seemed to notice. I got full marks in a test - Heather had passed her 'O' levels. I won the English Prize - Sandra had got into university. I felt invisible, like someone had turned a machine on me, and I'd disappeared. Even the boys would only speak to me to ask if Heather or Sandra were seeing anyone. It wasn't deliberate. Even when I got this job, the letter came the day before Sandra's wedding. But Phil's different. He notices me. He notices how I dress. He doesn't know Heather. He couldn't care less about Sandra. He notices me. Yes, of course, I know he's married. I'm under no illusions. Maybe he'll leave her; maybe he won't. Maybe this is forever or just for now. Maybe he's the one or just the first one. I don't know, and I don't care. I just like how he makes me feel.

TRAVIS

Thank God I met Lisa. I was starting to think I'd lost it—the old pulling power. I mean, I love Barbara and everything, but Lisa doesn't judge me. She doesn't say "Oh, Phil" because I didn't take the bins out. "Oh, Phil." That's what Barbara says all the time. I don't pick my socks up, and it's "Oh, Phil." I fall asleep in front of the telly and I get "Oh, Phil." I have to work late... If she knew what I was doing when she thinks I'm working late, she'd really say it. Lisa's nice, though. A bit clingy at times, but there are other compensations. Anyway, she'd stop that if she knew I didn't like it. She'd do anything for me. I'll tell her if she doesn't. Or finish it. I never said it was forever. She knows the score.

Blackout

(The lights come back up and the other teachers are staring at LISA and TRAVIS)

TRAVIS

The lying bastard!

BELLINGHAM

He was right last time.

TRAVIS

What's that supposed to mean?

BELLINGHAM

Nothing. Just saying, that's all.

TRAVIS

Me and Lisa? You're joking, aren't you? Lisa? Oh, come on! I'm married. Hudd's probably seen us having lunch together. As friends, before you say anything.

PALMER

Does Barbara think so? Does she even know?

TRAVIS

Barbara knows all she needs to know. You're only jealous.

PALMER

Of you trying to wreck your marriage? I don't think so.

LISA

It's true.

TRAVIS

Lisa...

LISA

I'm sorry, Phil. But you sounded like you were ashamed of me, and I can't stand that. It's true.

MRS. STEIN

Oh, Phil.

TRAVIS

Don't say that! Look, we're grown-ups. We're your colleagues, you know, not your pupils. What we do outside school is nothing to do with you, just like you and your husband.

MRS. STEIN

There's no call for that. You're supposed to be setting an example. Lisa, I'm surprised at you.

LISA

I'm not. Not really. I didn't think anyone knew.

TRAVIS

Well, I can't imagine Alastair keeping it to himself.

PALMER

Now wait a minute...!

LISA

Stop it! I'm sorry we've let you down, Christine, but we're still locked in. I want to get out more than ever now.

TRAVIS

I know what you mean there.

PALMER

Yes, Phil. Your wife will be worried.

TRAVIS

That's enough! I bet you put that little shit up to this.

PALMER

Not me. Can't stand the lad.

BELLINGHAM

He must be out there laughing at all this.

LISA

Laughing? What do you mean?

BELLINGHAM

He must be doing this for something. I think we all agree that Matthew Hudd is a lot of things, but stupid isn't one of them.

MRS. STEIN

You mean he's doing this for his own personal entertainment? That's awful!

PALMER

No more than making rats run round a maze. I think he's experimenting.

LISA

Then maybe he hasn't finished yet.

PALMER

Not finished?

LISA

He's had his laugh at Christine's expense and mine and Phil's. What about you and Stephen?

PALMER

There's nothing to tell.

LISA

He could make something up.

BELLINGHAM

In that case, I'm definitely going to break that door down!

MRS. STEIN

Wait! Just calm down, all of you. Maybe this is what he wants. Maybe he wants us at each other's throats. Or maybe he'd just like to see if we'll panic.

TRAVIS

So, what do you suggest?

MRS. STEIN

That we do nothing.

LISA

Nothing?

MRS. STEIN

Nothing. Let's just sit down and wait. I mean, Matthew Hudd is seventeen, and young people of that age are not noted for having long attention spans. If he's trying to entertain himself, then let's bore him. Let's just wait him out.

(Pause)

MRS. STEIN

Come on. Sit down, all of you.

(They all sit down. There is a long pause during which they glance around nervously at each other, the floor, the ceiling, anywhere but the door. They are all clearly very twitchy. After a while, PALMER gets up and starts to wander around.)

TRAVIS

Sit down, Alastair. You're making me nervous.

PALMER

My backside was getting numb.

(As he passes the door, PALMER quickly crouches and picks something up, standing up and carrying on as if nothing had happened. BELLINGHAM has seen, though and is out of his seat like a shot.)

BELLINGHAM

What is it?

PALMER

What's what?

BELLINGHAM

You picked something up. What was it?

PALMER

No, I didn't!

BELLINGHAM

Yes, you did. I saw you. It was another note, wasn't it?

PALMER

I didn't pick anything up.

BELLINGHAM

Show it to me.

MRS. STEIN

Leave him alone, Stephen.

BELLINGHAM

He knows it's about him. That's why he won't show us. Come on, Alastair. What's your secret?

MRS. STEIN

Leave him!

BELLINGHAM

Fair's fair, Christine. You've had your turn. Now it's Alastair's.

TRAVIS

I agree with Stephen. He had his little laugh at us. Hand it over, Alastair.

PALMER

There is NO NOTE!

TRAVIS

Do you want me to take it from you?

LISA

Phil, no!

(But TRAVIS is already on his feet and has PALMER by the lapels of his jacket.)

TRAVIS

Come on, Alastair. We're all friends here.

(There is a pause, then a terrified PALMER hands over a crumpled scrap of paper. TRAVIS reads it and laughs.)

TRAVIS

You should have read it before you hid it, Alastair. It's not about you at all.

(BELLINGHAM freezes)

PALMER

Well, read it then, Phil. Let's not have any secrets.

TRAVIS

"Ask Mr. Bellingham whether he prefers Teachers."

Blackout

INTERLUDE

(For this interlude, BELLINGHAM mimes having a bottle in one hand and a glass in the other. He takes frequent drinks from the glass, occasionally topping up from the bottle and gradually becomes drunker, but as a seasoned drinker, not outrageously so.)

BELLINGHAM

Of course, I like a drink; you would, too, if you worked in this school. No respect. No manners. And that's just the teachers. The kids are worse. Don't appreciate what we're doing this for. We've passed our exams; we've got jobs -thankless ones, but jobs just the same. I could work in a private school if I wanted to. Trouble is, they wouldn't know a decent teacher if they fell over one. Yes, I've applied for jobs, and no, I haven't got them, but that's their lack of taste; it's no fault of mine. So I teach here with idiotic liberals who want to help the kids. Well, let me tell you, the kids don't want our help. If they wanted help, they'd help themselves. All they want to do is pass their days and leave at the end of them. I mean, don't we all? And a little drink helps me unwind. There's no one else to talk to, and you know where you are with a bottle. It's not against the law, and I'd never drive.

Blackout

(When the lights come up, BELLINGHAM is sober but frozen to the spot. There is a pause. Then PALMER starts to laugh.)

BELLINGHAM

What? WHAT?

PALMER

"Teachers", eh? That's whisky, isn't it? It's all coming out today!

BELLINGHAM

He didn't mean that! He meant (*thinking fast*) do I get on with my colleagues!

TRAVIS

I think you're clutching straws there, Stephen, probably in more ways than one.

BELLINGHAM

He's a liar.

LISA

Don't worry, Stephen. We won't tell anyone.

BELLINGHAM

Tell anyone what?

MRS. STEIN

Just as long as you don't drink in school. You don't, do you?

PALMER

Of course, he does. He's always nipping off to the Black Lion at lunchtime.

BELLINGHAM

I do not!

PALMER

Why do you keep your desk locked? What's in it?

BELLINGHAM

You know what the kids are like!

LISA

Maybe you should think about getting some help.

BELLINGHAM

Maybe you should think about minding your own damn business!

TRAVIS

Don't start on her.

LISA

I can handle myself, Phil; I don't need your help.

TRAVIS

Suit yourself.

LISA

Perhaps I should start doing just that.

TRAVIS

And what's that supposed to mean?

LISA

I'm supposed to stop everything and run when you call. I'm not one of the kids. You can't tell me what to do. I had a life before you, Phil, and I'm going to have one again.

TRAVIS

I'm going to murder that Hudd.

MRS. STEIN

He's only told us the truth.

(Pause)

TRAVIS

But how does he know?

MRS. STEIN

I would imagine the signs are there to see if you look. We said he was intelligent.

PALMER

So you're on his side now.

MRS. STEIN

It's not a question of sides. He's set us all against each other and how? He's told all the little skeletons in our cupboards, and we've done the rest. It's amazing. You see people - work with them – every day, and think you know them, but really you don't know them at all.

LISA

Maybe that's his point.

BELLINGHAM

But we don't know Alastair yet, do we? He's the only one Hudd hasn't picked on.

PALMER

It could just be that I've got nothing to hide.

BELLINGHAM

You didn't seem to think so when that last note came through. In fact, you seemed very keen to get it before anyone else.

TRAVIS

Yes. Come on, Alastair, why don't you tell us before Hudd does?

PALMER

He can't tell you anything.

BELLINGHAM

Oh, I think he can.

MRS. STEIN

Stop that, Stephen, Phil. Why don't we just go back to trying to find a way out of here? I don't know about you, but I don't fancy being stuck in here all over Easter.

LISA

Won't the caretaker check at the end of the day?

MRS. STEIN

Of course! Why didn't we think of that?

LISA

I've only just remembered.

MRS. STEIN

What time is it?

BELLINGHAM

Twenty past four.

MRS. STEIN

We were due to finish at five. Forty minutes.

PALMER

I hate to put a damper on this, but I've sometimes wondered if Old Hargreaves checks here at all.

MRS. STEIN

What makes you say that?

PALMER

I shouldn't really say this, but it seems to be the day for confessions. I had the last lesson in here before Christmas and forgot to lock up. It nagged over Christmas, and I nearly came back a couple of times, but I thought, well, never mind, Hargreaves'll check. I made sure I was here first after the break, but the door was still unlocked. What's more, the bin hadn't been emptied, and it certainly hadn't been cleaned.

MRS. STEIN

I must say, I've noticed that about the bin, too.

BELLINGHAM

So we could be stuck here. That's it. I'm breaking the door down. Phil?

TRAVIS

I'm with you.

MRS. STEIN

I can't authorise that.

BELLINGHAM

Good. No one's asking you to. Look the other way if you want. We won't tell.

(BELLINGHAM and TRAVIS head for the door. As they do so, BELLINGHAM spots something on the floor.)

BELLINGHAM

Oh, look! Oh, Alastair.

PALMER

No! Give me that!

BELLINGHAM

(Reading) "Why does Mrs. Palmer wear dark glasses in winter?"

Blackout

INTERLUDE

PALMER

I love my wife. I love her dearly, but sometimes... the kids here... well, the biggest mistake ever was to abolish the cane. I mean, I don't support indiscriminate beatings. That's barbaric, positively Victorian. But occasionally... You only have to look at them, hear them, to know that they only understand one language. Apart from Anglo-Saxon, I mean. It's all about who's the hardest. Who can beat who up. Who's the cock of the school. If they gave GCSEs for fighting, we'd be top of the league table. It should be us, the teachers, who are cocks of the school. I get angry, and I know I shouldn't, and I take it home with me, and I know I shouldn't do that either. Sometimes I just catch a look in Dora's eye, which reminds me of a look I got from one of the fourth years, which said, "I haven't done my homework, and I'm not going to. What are you going to do about it?" And I hit her. Not often. Not really hard. And I hate myself. It's the one thing I said I'd never do, and it's the one thing Dora should never forgive, but she does. And each time, I think she'll walk on me, but she doesn't. If she ever did, I'd never forgive myself. That would be it for me. Maybe if my early retirement comes through.... God, I need a holiday.

Blackout

(The lights come up, and the rest of the teachers are staring accusingly at PALMER. He crumples into a chair.)

BELLINGHAM

He hits her! My God. He hits her.

MRS. STEIN

Do you, Alastair? Do you hit your wife?

TRAVIS

And they call me Psycho.

PALMER

You don't understand.

BELLINGHAM

Too right. You're pathetic, Alastair. Absolutely pathetic. No wonder you didn't want us to know.

LISA

(Tentatively approaching PALMER) Is it true, Alastair?

TRAVIS

Of course, it's true. Everything else was, wasn't it?

LISA

I wasn't asking you. Alastair?

PALMER

(Standing up) It's not like you think.

LISA

(Shrinking back) GET AWAY FROM ME!

PALMER

Lisa... it's not like that! Three times, maybe four... Dora understands. I can't help it.

MRS. STEIN

But you can't even remember how often. It doesn't matter whether you can help it or not. I've got the pupils and the rest of the staff to think of. If you can't control yourself with your own wife... you're finished here.

PALMER

It's not me! It's this place! Look at you all. Stephen drinks. Christine, your marriage has fallen apart. Lisa and Phil. What drove you together? No-one's perfect! I'd never touch anyone else here. You just want to make me into the villain, so you don't have to....

(Long pause. PALMER looks from one of his colleagues to another. It begins to dawn on him that his last speech was an error of judgement.)

BELLINGHAM

Don't you dare try and bring us to your level. We've got our faults but not like you. I've never hit anyone in my life.

MRS. STEIN

I was the victim in my marriage. My sympathies are with Dora.

PALMER

I didn't mean it like that! Think about it....

TRAVIS

I think you'd better just shut up.

PALMER

(Who is now walking the fine line between sanity and desperation) What about your wife, Phil? Aren't you hurting her? You mightn't hit her but is what you're doing any better?

TRAVIS

(Making a lunge for PALMER) I'll bloody kill him!

(PALMER takes a step back and stumbles over a chair. He falls to the floor. TRAVIS takes a pace towards him, but BELLINGHAM restrains him.)

BELLINGHAM

Leave him, Phil. The floor's where he belongs.

TRAVIS

Get OFF me!

LISA

(Quietly) I wonder if he knew this would happen.

MRS. STEIN

Who?

LISA

Matthew Hudd. I wonder if he knew.

PALMER

(Leaping to his feet) Hudd! *(He runs to the door)* This is his fault! I'll kill him! *(As he reaches the door, he stops dead. He stands, staring at the floor. There is a pause. Then he starts to laugh)* It's another one! Another note! *(Shouts at the door)* But there aren't any of us LEFT!

LISA

(Screams) Don't read it! *(Quieter)* Please. I don't want any more.

(TRAVIS goes to put a consoling arm around her shoulder, but she shrugs him off. PALMER is still holding the note, laughing to himself. MRS. STEIN goes over to him and takes the note from him.)

MRS. STEIN

(Reading) "I unlocked the door fifteen minutes ago. Didn't you check?" We're free to go.

BELLINGHAM

And all we have to do is face each other again. That's what he wanted.

TRAVIS

I'll get him for this. I swear I'll....

LISA

What for? For telling the truth? We're the ones who have got it all wrong, Phil, not him. I think we were safer in here.

MRS. STEIN

Then that's what it means.

BELLINGHAM

What?

MRS. STEIN

There's another bit to the note. It says, "Who goes first?"

(They all look at each other, then look at the door.

No-one moves.)

CURTAIN

Crossing the Border

A One Act Play

CAST IN ORDER OF APPEARANCE

YOUNG WOMAN

MAN

OLD WOMAN

PORTER

The action takes place on the platform of a railway station.

As the curtain opens, the stage is in darkness.

Gradually, the lights fade up to reveal a stage empty apart from a bench.

This could be any small railway station anywhere. Certainly, the YOUNG WOMAN sitting on the bench has the air of someone waiting for something. She is in her twenties, pretty enough but not dressed in an excessively glamorous way. She looks, in fact, like most travellers.

After a second or two, THE MAN enters. His age is hard to determine, but he is youngish. He is dressed in a green waterproof coat, under which camouflaged trousers and boots can be seen. It is unclear whether this is uniform or fashion.

THE MAN looks round for a second or two to take in his surroundings; then he spots THE YOUNG WOMAN. There is a moment's uncomfortable pause while he is uncertain as to how, or indeed even if, he should approach her.

Eventually, sensing that someone is behind her, she turns and sees him.

YOUNG WOMAN

Oh!

MAN

Sorry. I didn't mean to startle you

YOUNG WOMAN

You didn't. Well, no, you did, but only because I didn't know there was anyone there.

MAN

I haven't been here long. Miserable place, isn't it?

YOUNG WOMAN

They always are, though, stations. Don't you find that?

MAN

I suppose so. You'd think they'd give it a lick of paint, though. Or at least put in some decent lighting. I mean, you can hardly see anything, can you?

YOUNG WOMAN

I'm not sure how much I want to see. There's probably rats and all sorts round here.

MAN

Actually, I was only wondering if you knew what time the next train is due.

YOUNG WOMAN

I'm sorry, I don't. I was about to ask you the same thing.

MAN

I wonder if there's a timetable around here somewhere.

YOUNG WOMAN

I haven't seen one.

MAN

I'll just have a quick look.

(THE MAN walks to the exit r., but when he reaches it, he pauses. He stands still for a moment as if he has forgotten why he went there. Then, still looking slightly confused, comes back.)

YOUNG WOMAN

Did you find one?

MAN

Find one what?

YOUNG WOMAN

A timetable.

MAN

There wasn't one.

YOUNG WOMAN

You didn't go very far.

MAN

I...I remembered that I didn't see one.

YOUNG WOMAN

There must be a train soon. I mean, if there are two of us waiting now....

MAN

I suppose so.

YOUNG WOMAN

If it was going to be delayed, they'd have made an announcement, wouldn't they?

MAN

Probably.

YOUNG WOMAN

I'm glad, really. I wouldn't have fancied waiting here on my own.

MAN

You'd think the staff would look after the place a bit better. Mind you, come to think of it, I haven't seen any staff.

YOUNG WOMAN

No. It's always like this at night. My local station never has anyone there at night. You could get away without paying. I always pay, though. There'd be staff there if I didn't.

MAN

That'd be about right. Wait a minute. Did you just say it was night?

YOUNG WOMAN

Yes. Why?

MAN

I just thought…no. Never mind. God, it's miserable here. Cold too.

YOUNG WOMAN

It'll be warmer on the train.

MAN

If the bloody train ever gets here. What time is it now?

YOUNG WOMAN

(looks at her wrist) Sorry. I haven't got my watch on.

MAN

(looking at his wrist) Mine's stopped. I knew I should have got it checked before I left. *(Tuts)* Look at that. The glass is broken too. I must have hit it on something.

YOUNG WOMAN

This is typical of me. I never go anywhere without my watch and the one time I need it….

MAN

I don't suppose it matters. Without a timetable, we don't know what time the train's due anyway.

YOUNG WOMAN

Funny there being no timetable. Did you look that way? *(Points off l.)*

MAN

No.

YOUNG WOMAN

I'll go and look.

(She goes to the exit t., but as she does so, an OLD WOMAN enters.)

YOUNG WOMAN

Oh!

OLD WOMAN

Sorry, dear. Is this where you wait?

YOUNG WOMAN

It seems to be. There's a bench if you want to sit down.

OLD WOMAN

Thank you. I am rather tired. *(Notices THE MAN)* Oh, good afternoon.

MAN

Good....afternoon? Is it only the afternoon?

OLD WOMAN

Well, it was when I got here. I've been wandering round a bit. It's probably later than that now. Please don't let me interrupt you. I'll just rest here.

YOUNG WOMAN

Oh, we're not together. We've just met.

OLD WOMAN

I'm sorry. I just thought.... Are you travelling to the same place?

MAN

I suppose we must be.

OLD WOMAN

Perhaps we all are. It'll be nice to have some company. I hate travelling on my own. You meet some very strange people on trains sometimes.

YOUNG WOMAN

How do you know we're not? Strange, I mean.

OLD WOMAN

I think I'd be able to tell.

MAN

Well, I've broken my watch and don't know how, and this young lady hasn't brought hers at all. Neither of us can find a timetable. I think that's about as strange as we get.

OLD WOMAN

If you don't get any stranger than that, I think we'll all get along very well. Are you in the army?

MAN

(looking at his uniform) The army? Yes. I am.

OLD WOMAN

I suppose you've been home on leave and are going back to join your regiment.

MAN

Yes. That's it.

OLD WOMAN

Where's your kit bag?

MAN

My kit bag? *(looks around)* I seem to have misplaced it.

OLD WOMAN

They won't be very pleased about that.

MAN

No. Maybe it'll turn up.

OLD WOMAN

You should try the lost property office. I lost an umbrella once. *(Laughs at the memory)* My husband was furious. He'd only just bought it for my birthday…or was it Christmas? Luckily someone had handed it in.

YOUNG WOMAN

Isn't your husband with you?

OLD WOMAN

No. *(Confused for a moment)* No. He isn't.

YOUNG WOMAN

You must have been married for a long time.

OLD WOMAN

Forty-nine years! We're having a party for our Golden Wedding next year. My daughter's organising it. I didn't want one. I don't like fuss. But she insisted.

YOUNG WOMAN

What's your husband's name?

OLD WOMAN

George? Is it George? No, it's Geoffrey. What a thing to forget. I must be going senile. Wait till I tell him.

MAN

I don't suppose you noticed a timetable at all?

OLD WOMAN

No, I don't think I did.

MAN

We've been trying to find one.

OLD WOMAN

Well, the train must turn up soon, mustn't it?

YOUNG WOMAN

Maybe two will turn up at the same time.

OLD WOMAN

I don't think trains do that, do they? Buses do, but not trains.

MAN

I'd just settle for one. *(He goes to the front of the stage and listens)* No sign. Sometimes you hear the track sort of twang when there's a train coming, but there's nothing.

YOUNG WOMAN

There must be someone we can ask, surely.

OLD WOMAN

Maybe the station isn't staffed at night. I can't say I blame them. Who'd want to work here?

(There is a long pause.)

MAN

(Finally) That's it! I've had enough. I'm going to find out what's going on.

(He heads to the exit r., pausing briefly to look back at the other, then exits.

After a moment or two, during which the two women look anxiously at each other, THE MAN returns, obviously very agitated.)

MAN

This has got to be somebody's idea of a joke.

YOUNG WOMAN

(Going to him) What is it? What's the matter?

MAN

Either I'm going bonkers or someone's playing a trick on us.

YOUNG WOMAN

Why? What did you find?

MAN

Nothing.

YOUNG WOMAN

What, no timetable?

MAN

No, nothing. There's nothing there. It's just black.

YOUNG WOMAN

It's probably just dark.

MAN

(Suddenly angry) No. It's not dark! There's nothing there!

YOUNG WOMAN

(Leading him back to the bench) Come on, sit down. Come on, calm down and tell us what you saw.

MAN

I didn't see anything because there's nothing there to see! No light, nothing. There's always some light, isn't there? But there's nothing there!

OLD WOMAN

Maybe your eyes needed to get used to it.

MAN

There's nothing there! Go and look yourself. *(He goes back to the r. exit and calls)* Come on! You've had your joke. Come out and explain yourself!

(While he is at the r. exit and the women are watching him, someone else enters l. This is the man we will come to know as THE PORTER. He could be any age and is dressed in a white jacket and black trousers. He stands and watches while THE MAN shouts.)

MAN

This has gone far enough! There are women here and they're scared.

PORTER

They don't look very scared to me, though someone does.

MAN

Who are you?

PORTER

You called.

(Angrily THE MAN crosses over to THE PORTER.)

MAN

I asked you who you are.

PORTER

And I answered you. Who would you like me to be?

MAN

I'd like you to be someone who can tell us just what, in God's name, is going on around here.

PORTER

I might very well be just that.

MAN

Are you?

PORTER

Or I might not. Depends how nicely you ask.

MAN

Don't play games with me. Where the hell are we?

PORTER

No need to be rude. Ask nicely.

MAN

Why you…!

YOUNG WOMAN

(intervening) I'm sorry. We've had a bit of a night of it in one way or another. Please could you tell us where we are?

PORTER

Oh, she's good. I like her. As to where you are…I'd have thought it was obvious. You're in the station.

MAN

Then where are the bloody trains?

PORTER

Language. The train will be here soon enough.

MAN

And when exactly is that? What time?

PORTER

What does it matter? You haven't a watch between you. Time is irrelevant.

MAN

Aren't you supposed to be paid to be helpful? Because you're not.

PORTER

If you're going to be like that, I shall leave you to it. You're not the only people I have to see to, you know.

YOUNG WOMAN

You mean there are other people here?

PORTER

People travel the route you are taking all the time. I wouldn't worry about them too much, though.

MAN

Look, while you're talking in riddles, we're getting scared out of our wits here. Do you know it's just black out there?

PORTER

Oh, I think you'll find that there's always light if you know where to look.

MAN

At the end of the tunnel, I suppose.

PORTER

Very good! I'm glad to see you've kept your sense of humour.

YOUNG WOMAN

Please. If you know what's going on, will you just tell us? Isn't the train ready yet?

PORTER

The train's ready. I'm just not sure if you're ready for the train.

MAN

What does that mean?

PORTER

That, I'm afraid, is something you're going to have to work out for yourselves.

YOUNG WOMAN

I bet there are cameras somewhere. We're on that TV show, aren't we?

PORTER

You'll have to go a bit deeper than that. Now, I'm sorry, but I really must go. If I were you, I'd just think about how you got here.

YOUNG WOMAN

Will you be back?

PORTER

Oh, I'll be back all right. You're not going anywhere without me.

(He exits.)

MAN

Hey! Come back!

YOUNG WOMAN

Leave him. He said he'd be back.

MAN

But he didn't tell us anything.

OLD WOMAN

He told us to think about how we got here.

MAN

How we got here? What does that mean? We know how we got here.

OLD WOMAN

How?

(Pause)

MAN

Well, I don't know about you, but I....

OLD WOMAN

You don't know, do you?

MAN

Of course, I do.

OLD WOMAN

Then tell us how.

MAN

I... I don't know. I thought I did, but I don't.

OLD WOMAN

Neither do I. I started thinking about it when he said. I don't remember coming here at all. I remember being her, of course, and I remember not being here, but I don't remember getting here.

YOUNG WOMAN

Neither do I.

MAN

Isn't that the strangest… This is getting weirder and weirder. Do you think they've done something to us?

OLD WOMAN

What, drugged the drinks in the buffet? I haven't seen one, let alone been there.

MAN

Well, they've done something.

OLD WOMAN

Who? Who are they?

MAN

Whoever he works for. Someone's brought us here for something.

OLD WOMAN

Isn't that a bit paranoid?

MAN

At the moment, it's the best I can do.

YOUNG WOMAN

What if there's something wrong with us?

MAN

Of course, there's something wrong with us. We're stuck at a station in the middle of the bloody night, and we don't know why!

OLD WOMAN

Don't take it out on her.

MAN

Well, it was a silly thing to say.

OLD WOMAN

Was it? That man didn't look like a railway porter. He looked more like a hospital porter. Did he say he worked here?

MAN

Well... no.

OLD WOMAN

Then maybe he works somewhere else.

YOUNG WOMAN

Where?

OLD WOMAN

A hospital? A while ago, I couldn't remember my husband's name, and I said then I must be going senile. Maybe I am, and I'm going somewhere to get help.

MAN

You might be, but there's nothing wrong with me.

OLD WOMAN

You can't remember getting here.

MAN

Apart from that.

OLD WOMAN

I think things would be easier if you were honest with us. If we all were.

MAN

What are you saying? That I'm a liar?

OLD WOMAN

Not a liar. Just not honest. Where were you going?

MAN

To rejoin my regiment. I told you that.

OLD WOMAN

No, I told you that. You agreed. Where is your regiment based?

MAN

I can't tell you that.

OLD WOMAN

Why? Because you're not allowed to, or because you don't know?

MAN

I... I... I don't know. There. I've said it now. Are you happy?

OLD WOMAN

Not really. I'm not happy about any of this. But since you've been honest with me, I'll be honest with you. I don't know where I'm going, either. I don't know where I'm going or why my Geoffrey isn't with me. We've not gone anywhere apart since the war.

YOUNG WOMAN

I don't know, either. That must be what that man meant. If we work out where we've come from, we might be able to work out where we're going.

(Staging note: As the characters begin to talk about themselves, a change comes over the way they speak. Up until now, they have been speaking in neutral accents, but as they start to talk about themselves, their real accents begin to come through, Liverpool for the MAN, London for the YOUNG WOMAN and Yorkshire for the OLD WOMAN. This change should be gradual, though, not sudden.)

MAN

I know where I'm from. Liverpool. Allerton. I was born there, went to school there and had my first kiss there in a bus shelter when I was fifteen and her name was Susan, and it was great. I've had five girlfriends since then and lost my virginity to the second. That wasn't quite so great. I'm still single, and I live with my mam. I went on the dole when I left school because I trained as a brickie and didn't like it. Then I joined the army. I remember it all.

OLD WOMAN

Apart from why you're here.

MAN

You can't have everything.

YOUNG WOMAN

I'm from London. The East End. It's just like it is on the telly, only less happens. I went into modelling because everyone said I should. Even when I was little, they all said to my mum that I should be on the adverts. She tried that, but I screamed all the time at the audition so they wouldn't have me. That's what my mum said. I went into modelling, and I do magazines and catalogues. I don't do no Page 3 stuff or nothing like that. Alan's my boyfriend and sort of my manager and he always comes with me on shoots. I think he likes to watch.

OLD WOMAN

Is that where you're going now? On a shoot?

YOUNG WOMAN

I don't think so. I haven't got my things. Or Alan.

OLD WOMAN

Then where are you going?

YOUNG WOMAN

I don't know. Do you think he was from a hospital? That man? Only some of the other girls have had problems, stress and that. Eating problems. One girl, Jenni with an 'I', always made herself sick before a shoot. But I never done nothing like that. I don't do drugs, either. Alan wouldn't let me. Not that I'd want to.

OLD WOMAN

Well, something must have happened. There must be some reason why you can't remember why you're here.

YOUNG WOMAN

What about you? What can you remember?

OLD WOMAN

I can remember lots of things, but then I've seen lots of things. I don't remember many early things, well, not really early things, but it was a long time ago. I remember my wedding, though, as if it were yesterday. We live in a little village in Yorkshire, Dalton, it's called. We grew up together, and everyone said we'd get married one day, and we did. There was never anyone else. I was seventeen, but no-one said I was too young. It was 1939, and everyone was saying there was a war coming. They all knew Geoffrey would get called up, so we got married. I wanted him to have a wife to come home to, not a girlfriend.

YOUNG WOMAN

But he came through it okay?

OLD WOMAN

More or less. It was a horrible time, not knowing where he was half the time or how he was. But he got shot in the leg in '42, and they sent him home to me. He always had a bit of a limp, especially when it was damp. He worked in his dad's shop and took it over when his dad died. We had three kids and eight grandchildren. I'm a great-grandmother now.

YOUNG WOMAN

Maybe you're going to see one of your grandchildren.

OLD WOMAN

Not without my Geoffrey, I'm not. He dotes on those kids.

MAN

Then where are you going?

OLD WOMAN

I don't know. Funny you being in the army and me saying that about Geoffrey. 'Course, you won't have seen any combat, will you?

MAN

I have.

OLD WOMAN

Where?

MAN

I'm sure I have.

OLD WOMAN

Ireland?

MAN

No. I never went to Ireland. But I joined up because of a war.

YOUNG WOMAN

Iraq?

MAN

Where?

YOUNG WOMAN

You must have heard of Iraq.

MAN

(with a shrug) There was a war. Me and Eric both signed up together. Susan didn't want him to go... they got married, did I tell you? We both went because it was a wage. She had a baby on the way, and he wanted to earn proper money. I went with him because he was my mate and it seemed like the right thing to do. They gave us guns and showed us how to use them. It must have happened. I can still smell the gun oil. And the sea... I can still smell the sea. I... I can't remember any more. Just... there's something about a bird.

YOUNG WOMAN

A girl?

MAN

No, a *bird* bird... no, it's gone. Can we talk about something else?

YOUNG WOMAN

(To the OLD WOMAN) You were telling us about your Geoffrey. Has he still got the shop?

OLD WOMAN

No, love. We sold it. Not long ago. Geoffrey thought about retiring when he got to sixty-five, but he just kept going. It never made a fortune, especially when all the supermarkets started opening, but it did us, and people liked going in there, so he kept it on. But he had a heart attack, four years ago it was. It wasn't a bad one. I didn't think I was going to lose him or anything, but it scared him. We sold up and moved into a little flat nearby.

YOUNG WOMAN

It must be great to be with someone for so long.

OLD WOMAN

It is. We've had our moments, same as everyone else, but mostly it has been great, yes.

YOUNG WOMAN

Alan and I argue all the time, but we always make up. I like the making-up.

MAN

I bet you do.

YOUNG WOMAN

Not like that! I just like it when it feels like he loves me again.

OLD WOMAN

I've never felt like Geoffrey didn't love me. Even when we've argued.

YOUNG WOMAN

Was he really handsome? You know, when he was young? I mean, he probably still is, but....

OLD WOMAN

We made a lovely couple. That's what everyone said. A lot of girls had their eye on him, I can tell you. But I got him. Only thing is....

MAN

What?

OLD WOMAN

I... I can't remember what he looks like. I try to picture his face, but I can't. Silly old fool. Sooner they get me to this hospital, the better.

MAN

You still think that's where we're going?

OLD WOMAN

Can't think of anything else that makes sense. He said it was something to do with our memories, that porter. Maybe it's a place that deals with amnesia.

MAN

That could be it, you know. Some sort of trauma clinic.

YOUNG WOMAN

What sort of trauma?

MAN

If we knew that, we wouldn't need to go. Mind you, that's not a bad idea. Why don't we find out what trauma, then we can just go home?

YOUNG WOMAN

Wouldn't it be best to let the professionals do it? I mean, the train must be here soon. I don't fancy finding out what's wrong with me on a railway station, miles from anywhere, with no one here to help me.

MAN

We'll help you.

YOUNG WOMAN

But I don't know you. No offence.

MAN

You don't know them either.

YOUNG WOMAN

But they know what they're doing. It might be dangerous.

MAN

How can it be dangerous? Whatever's happened to you has already happened and you survived, didn't you?

YOUNG WOMAN

Only by not remembering.

MAN

Well, I want to try.

YOUNG WOMAN

Don't. Please.

MAN

Don't worry. If I try and remember and nothing happens to me, you'll know it's okay, won't you?

YOUNG WOMAN

But what if something does happen to you?

MAN

Then you'll know not to try.

YOUNG WOMAN

What are you going to do?

MAN

I'm going to talk to you both. Tell you what I remember. I want you to ask me questions. Help me fill in the gaps.

OLD WOMAN

If you're sure.

MAN

I don't know about sure.

YOUNG WOMAN

Then don't do it.

MAN

No. Let's go. I remember signing up for the army. Me and Eric went together. We both dressed dead smart, you know? Suits and everything. Got them down the Oxfam. Mine fitted, but Eric's didn't. We had a medical and we both passed. We signed up there and then. I remember saying goodbye to everyone. We had a night in the Lion and Unicorn. I didn't want to drink too much, but Eric got off his head. He was sick twice on the train the next day.

OLD WOMAN

Which train?

MAN

The train to camp. Basic training. Marlow! I've just remembered the name of the sergeant who drilled us. Sergeant Marlow. What a bastard he was. He pushed us and pushed us, and I remember thinking, if he shouts at me once more, I'm going to plant one on him. But I didn't because I wanted to be there.

OLD WOMAN

I thought you said you went because of Eric.

MAN

At first. But once I got there, I thought, this is it. This is what I want.

YOUNG WOMAN

Was it hard?

MAN

Had to be. There wasn't much time. We were there three weeks, then they sent us off.

OLD WOMAN

Off where?

MAN

To the war.

OLD WOMAN

Which war?

MAN

I'm trying to think.

YOUNG WOMAN

Was it the Gulf War? Is that where you went?

MAN

The Gulf War? What's that?

YOUNG WOMAN

The Gulf War. Saddam Hussein.

MAN

I don't think I've ever heard of it.

OLD WOMAN

Unless you don't remember.

MAN

Maybe that's it. Tell me about it.

YOUNG WOMAN

It was in the Middle East....

MAN

The Middle East? That's deserts and stuff, isn't it? I don't remember sand. I remember sea. We got off the boat and I went up to my knees in water. It was bloody freezing. It would have been hot in the Middle East, but it was cold, and we were scared.

YOUNG WOMAN

Don't. Don't go on if you don't want to.

MAN

No. It's coming back. There was grass and rocks. It wasn't a desert. We were scared, but nothing happened. We pitched camp for the night, but we didn't really sleep. We were wound up tight. We just passed round ciggies and tried to make jokes and waited for something to happen. But it didn't.

OLD WOMAN

Something must have happened.

MAN

Not then. This went on for a couple of days, then... Eric. Jesus, I remember. It was Eric. They got Eric.

YOUNG WOMAN

Who did?

MAN

(reliving it now) We can hear the guns, but we can't see them. You can see the bullets hit the ground and the rocks. The sarge is screaming at us to GET DOWN NOW! And most of the lads do, but Eric's frozen. He's just standing there, so I make a run for him. I try and knock him down, but he goes down anyway. He's been hit, and there's blood everywhere. Our lads are firing, and I can smell the smoke and Eric's trying to say something, but the guns are too loud. I'm thinking Susie'll never forgive me for this. He's soaked and I'm soaked and then... there's nothing.

OLD WOMAN

Nothing?

MAN

There's nothing else.

YOUNG WOMAN

Oh, you poor thing. That's terrible.

MAN

But I can't remember nothing else.

OLD WOMAN

I'm not surprised. Seeing your friend die like that.

MAN

But I want to remember the rest.

OLD WOMAN

It'll come. That came. The rest will come.

MAN

But that was supposed to cure me. Remembering was supposed to cure me. Where's that porter?

OLD WOMAN

What do you want him for?

MAN

I don't need to go anywhere now, do I? I've been through it all again. That's what they wanted. I can't remember nothing else, but, hey, that's my problem.

OLD WOMAN

I don't think it's as easy as that.

MAN

(bitterly) What else do they want? "You've remembered the worst thing that ever happened to you, lad. Now frig off and sort yourself out". You want to try it. It's great.

YOUNG WOMAN

Don't be like that.

MAN

How do you want me to be? What's the worst thing that ever happened to you? A broken nail? Come on, I've told you mine.

YOUNG WOMAN

Alan beat me up.

(Pause)

MAN

That's it? Your boyfriend beat you up?

YOUNG WOMAN

You don't understand. He's always been jealous. That's why he always had to go to the shoots with me. He's my manager and he sorts all the work out for me and that, but he doesn't like other men looking at me. He wants to stay around in case anyone tries it on. No-one ever does because they're all scared of him. I'm a bit scared of him too. He always says it's my own fault for being too beautiful. That's what he says. He says men are men and they can't help themselves. So, he's only looking out for me, isn't he?

MAN

Then why did he beat you up?

YOUNG WOMAN

Oh, it was a bit silly, really. I thought I'd get a picture done for his birthday. You know, a proper glamour one, nothing saucy. So, I booked in with a photographer we know, Darryl, and got myself all glammed up. It was brilliant. I was going to get a nice frame, an expensive one. But Alan found out. I hadn't even seen the contact sheet, but he found out. He was raving. He said Darryl was the worst of the lot and then he said... he said he'd make sure no-one wanted to look at me again. *(She starts to sob)* That's when he did it.

MAN

You don't have to go on.

YOUNG WOMAN

(furiously) You wanted to hear it! You wanted to hear, so shut up and bloody listen! *(She composes herself)* The first time he hit me, I didn't believe it, like it was happening to someone else. So I just stood there. Then he did it again, and I felt that. It wasn't a slap, either. He used his fist. I go down, but he pulls me up again by my blouse, and some of the buttons come off, and I can see them on the floor, and I'm thinking, that was expensive, that blouse. He keeps hitting me and I just sort of let him and wait for it to stop. Then it's dark and he's gone. I don't know when he went. Funny thing is, it doesn't hurt much. I'm sort of numb. But I want to see what he's done. The bedroom mirror's broken for some reason, so I sort of drag myself into the bathroom. There's a mirror on the medicine cabinet over the sink, so I pull myself up to have a look and... that's all I can remember. That's the worst thing that happened to me.

MAN

I'm sorry.

YOUNG WOMAN

You should be. You made me remember.

OLD WOMAN

Let's leave this now.

YOUNG WOMAN

Let's not. It's your turn now. What's the worst thing that's ever happened to you?

(Unnoticed by everyone, THE PORTER has entered.)

OLD WOMAN

I'm sorry. There isn't one.

YOUNG WOMAN

There must be. If that's why we're here, there must be something.

OLD WOMAN

Nothing. I'm just ordinary. I've had an ordinary life. Ups and downs like everyone. I'm just an ordinary woman.

PORTER

But that's not exactly true, is it?

MAN

What do you want?

PORTER

It's nearly time to go.

MAN

Go? Go where? We're not going anywhere.

PORTER

I wish I could say you had a choice.

MAN

You're going to make us, are you?

PORTER

It's not really a question of that. You just don't have a choice.

MAN

But we don't need to go. We've remembered, me and her, and this lady has nothing to remember.

PORTER

Well, as I said, that's not exactly true. What about Geoffrey's face?

OLD WOMAN

What about it? Have you been listening?

PORTER

You don't remember it, do you? Why not?

OLD WOMAN

I... I don't know.

PORTER

And that's not all you don't remember. You don't remember your stroke, do you?

OLD WOMAN

I don't know what you're talking about.

PORTER

Try and think a bit harder. You were in the kitchen....

OLD WOMAN

The kitchen..? I... oh, Lord, yes. Geoff had gone out to the garden, and I was shelling peas. I dropped the pan and couldn't pick it up. I couldn't feel anything. I can smell the chops under the grill and I'm hoping they don't burn. Then I'm in hospital and Geoff's sitting there. I think he's crying, and I want to tell him I'm alive, but I can't talk. I can't see his face. Why can't I see his face?

PORTER

Because this is the worst thing that ever happened to you. You died.

(Long pause)

OLD WOMAN

But I can't have done. I'm here. I'm talking to you. I can't be dead because I'm talking to you!

PORTER

You really don't get it, do you? Any of you? Let me spell it out for you. (*Points to each one in turn*)

You're dead, and you're dead, and you're dead. This isn't just any old waiting room. You're waiting for the Non-Stop service to the Pearly Gates, or the Brimstone Express.

MAN

You're lying. I'll see you lose your job for this.

PORTER

Oh really?

MAN

Really. How dare you come round here scaring us all? Are you insane?

PORTER

I'm perfectly sane. Most people have a job adjusting. You all had rather traumatic deaths so it's a bit harder for you.

MAN

We are not dead!

PORTER

Yes, you are.

MAN

I'm as alive as you.

PORTER

You say pot-ay-to and I say pot-ah-to. Look, you probably are as alive as me, but you're still dead if you get my meaning. You all need to think back a little bit more. You've remembered a lot, but not quite enough. You, for example. Why do you think there was so much blood on you and Eric? And you... *(To the YOUNG WOMAN)* What did you see in the mirror and what did you see in the cabinet? And you. *(To the OLD WOMAN)* You still haven't explained why you can't picture Geoffrey's face.

(*During the next lines, the characters are not speaking to each other or to THE PORTER, and as they speak, a train can be heard in the distance, getting ever nearer*)

OLD WOMAN

I want to talk to Geoff and tell him everything will be fine, but I can't get my mouth to work. Sounds come out, but I don't know if he can hear them or it's just me.

MAN

It's not a bird, it's Goose Green and Eric's speaking, but I can't hear him over the guns. I put my head lower to hear him, but all I can smell is his breath, and it smells like something that's died....

YOUNG WOMAN

I can see my face in the mirror, but it doesn't look like me. It's black and ugly and ruined. He's ruined my face and it was all I had....

OLD WOMAN

... and I open my mouth to speak again and all that comes out is spit, but I can't move my hand to wipe it away. And Geoff....

MAN

… And as I lower my head, there's another bang and it seems closer. It looks like Eric's started bleeding again, and it can't be because he's dead….

YOUNG WOMAN

… And I open the medicine cabinet and I can see the pain killers I keep in there for all the other times he's done this, only he's never done it so badly before….

OLD WOMAN

… And I want Geoff to help me, but he can't see me….

MAN

… And I look to see where the blood's coming from….

YOUNG WOMAN

… And the tablets taste bitter because I can't swallow them quickly enough….

OLD WOMAN

… He can't see me because he can't bear to. He's looking away and I'm slipping….

MAN

… And I can see that the blood's coming from me and I'm slipping…..

YOUNG WOMAN

… And I feel like going to sleep and I'm slipping….

PORTER

And the next thing you know, you're all here.

(By now, the sound of the train has reached a crescendo and THE PORTER has to shout to make himself heard)

PORTER

I wish I could tell you where you were all going, but I don't know myself. That's why I agreed to stay here. Still, half the fun's in the surprise, isn't it?

(Pause)

PORTER

All aboard!

Blackout

CURTAIN

Some of Us Are Looking At the Stars

A One Act Play

CAST IN ORDER OF APPEARANCE

DONNA WARREN

JACK NIXON

MARION NIXON

DAVID

SHEILA HARKER

ROSS HARKER

The play takes place on the top of a hill at night.

The time is the present day.

SCENE ONE

The stage is empty. No scenery is really necessary, except perhaps a backdrop of evening sky, suggesting that the action of the play takes place in the open air, up high on a hill, on a clear starry evening. If this is not possible, then the stage should be left completely empty and everything else conveyed by the actors.

When the curtains open, the stage remains empty for a moment or two, then DONNA WARREN enters. She is in her twenties and would normally be attractive, but as the play opens, she has been on the road for a while. Her clothes are quite scruffy and her hair lank. She enters cautiously, looking all round. Satisfied that there is no-one else around, she sits on the ground, exhausted. She starts to adjust the laces on her boots. As she does so, voices are heard off. DONNA freezes like a rabbit caught in the headlights of a car.

MALE VOICE

(off) I told you it wasn't far.

FEMALE VOICE

(off) Not far? I feel like I've walked for miles!

(DONNA, hearing that the voices are getting closer, gets to her feet and runs off. As she does so, the owners of the voices we have heard come into view. They are JACK and MARION NIXON, a middle-aged couple. They are dressed in almost identical costumes and seem to have paid a great deal of

money on all the best hiking gear, waterproof jackets, boots and matching woollen hats.

JACK has a spacious rucksack on his back.)

JACK

Anyway, we're here now. And just look at that view!

MARION

It's incredible! It's almost worth the walk.

JACK

Only almost?

MARION

It was a long way.

JACK

Well, if the view was only 'almost' worth the walk, the rest of tonight should make up for it.

MARION

I hope we haven't come all this way for nothing.

JACK

(Putting his arm around her) It will be worth it. I promise. This will be a night you'll never forget.

MARION

Really? I mean, I wouldn't want you to be disappointed. You've done this sort of thing before, but I....

JACK

Not another word. It doesn't matter how often I've done it. This is the first time I've done it with you and that makes it special.

MARION

Thank you, Jack. You're very sweet. I just hope I don't put a jinx on it or something.

JACK

Of course, you won't. Don't start thinking like that. Tonight's going to be wonderful. I can feel it.

(At that moment, DAVID enters. He is in his thirties/forties and dressed in black leather jacket, black T-shirt and black jeans. He passes by JACK and MARION, saying "Evening" as he does so. He goes to the other side of the stage and sits on the ground. He takes a book out of a pocket of his jacket and starts to read.)

JACK

Well, of all the...

MARION

(warning) Jack...

JACK

He's got a nerve. We were here first.

MARION

We don't own the hill, Jack. Let's just go somewhere else.

JACK

Certainly not. This is by far the best spot.

MARION

He's probably here for the same reason as we are. He probably won't be the last, either. If he's heard about it, and we've heard about it, I doubt if we're the only ones.

JACK

That's a depressing thought. The place could be swarming with people. It'll ruin everything.

MARION

Why? Will an audience spoil it?

JACK

Oh, I don't know. I'm just being selfish, I suppose. I just wanted us to have it all to ourselves.

MARION

I know you did. But it doesn't look like we're going to be able to. Let's at least try to be sociable, shall we? We're probably going to be sharing a hill with him all evening.

JACK

You're right, of course. *(He wanders over to DAVID.)* Good evening. Very mild, isn't it?

DAVID

(Putting his book down) It's August. It should be.

JACK

Yes. Well. I take it you're here for the same reason we are?

DAVID

That would depend on why you're here, wouldn't it? I mean, I'd imagine people come up onto this hill on summer evenings for all sorts of reasons. In couples.

JACK

What? Oh. No. That's not why we're here. I'm Jack Nixon, by the way, and this is my wife Marion. *(He beckons to MARION, who comes to join him.)*

DAVID

So why have you come here, Mr. Nixon? Are you just here to admire the view?

JACK

No, we're not, and I think you know that, Mr ....

DAVID

David will do.

(At that moment, more voices are heard off.)

WOMAN'S VOICE

Are you sure this is the right hill?

YOUNG MAN'S VOICE

It went this way. I'm sure.

DAVID

Here come the crowds. I don't suppose you've got any booze in that rucksack, have you, Mr. Nixon? We could have a party.

(The owners of the voices come into view. They are SHEILA HARKER, a worried-looking woman in her forties, and her son ROSS, a rather nervous young man in his mid to late teens.)

SHEILA

Oh.

DAVID

Come and join us. We were just thinking of having a party.

SHEILA

I think we're in the wrong place. I'm sorry.

DAVID

(Getting up and extending a welcoming hand to them) Not at all. I think you're in the right place. What do you think, Jack? Marion?

MARION

I really don't know.

DAVID

I think all six of us are here for the same reason.

JACK

Six?

DAVID

You can come out now.

(Nervously, DONNA emerges from where she has been hiding offstage.)

DAVID

(to DONNA) Sorry to startle you, but I could hear you moving around.

DONNA

You should have left me alone.

DAVID

Maybe. Anyway, now we're all here, let's have some introductions. I'm David, these are my new friends Jack and Marion Nixon, and you are..?

SHEILA

Sheila. Sheila Harker. This is my son Ross.

ROSS

(Quietly) Hi.

DAVID

(to DONNA) And what about you? Who are you?

DONNA

Mind your own business.

DAVID

Fair enough. I don't know about you lot, but I think we should make ourselves comfortable. It's going to be a long night.

(He sits on the ground. The others look at him for a moment, then JACK makes a move. He opens the rucksack and takes out two rolled-up off-cuts of carpet. He suddenly becomes aware that everyone is now looking at him, not DAVID.)

JACK

In case the grass was damp.

(As he places the pieces of carpet on the ground, and he and MARION make themselves comfortable on them, ROSS leads SHEILA to one side.)

ROSS

This wasn't a good idea, Mum.

SHEILA

Of course, it was.

ROSS

But all these people ....

SHEILA

You know what Dr. Theakston said. Don't you want to get better?

ROSS

Yes, I do, but ....

SHEILA

Then we'll stay. They all seem nice enough.

(SHEILA and ROSS come back and join the rest of the group. They, too, sit on the ground. Only DONNA stays on her own, standing to one side.)

DAVID

Seeing as we're all here for the same reason, I think it's probably a good idea if we get to know each other better, don't you?

MARION

Are we, though?

DAVID

Are we what?

MARION

Here for the same reason? We're all assuming we are, but....

DAVID

It's August the 4th.

JACK

We know the date. So what?

DAVID

That's a very significant date round here, isn't it? What if I were to say that strange things have been happening round here on August the 4th? What if I were to mention lights in the sky? Am I right?

(There is a murmur of assent from all but DONNA.)

DAVID

I thought so. I've never really believed in coincidence. I think we'll find the full story goes something like this. August 4th, 2022. Seven members of the local hiking club all see a bright light over Edgemoor Hill. As they draw closer, the light flies off at an incredible speed. It later turns out that several other people saw the lights that night too. A couple out driving their car near Edgemoor Hill nearly crash when bright lights appear in the sky over the road. Three other confirmed sightings that night. August 4th 2020 ....

JACK

How do you know all this?

DAVID

I'm interested.

MARION

You've certainly done your research.

DAVID

Maybe I'm a Man in Black.

SHEILA

A what?

ROSS

The Men in Black are supposed to appear at the sights were UFOs are seen, but no one knows who they are.

DAVID

Or will admit to knowing.

MARION

And that's what you are?

DAVID

(laughing) I only said maybe. Now I don't think that we're gathered here tonight because we're just curious about lights in the sky which appear on Edgemoor Hill every August 4th, are we? Jack, you and Marion were in the hiking club that night, weren't you?

JACK

How did you know?

DAVID

Just a guess. You've got all the gear.

JACK

But you haven't researched it very well, have you? I was there, but Marion was ill.

DAVID

And I'd guess that young Ross saw something too, but his mother didn't.

SHEILA

It's nonsense, of course, but....

ROSS

(vehemently) I saw it!

DAVID

Of course, you did. *(To DONNA)* And what about you, Miss Mystery? What are you doing here?

DONNA

I don't know what you're talking about. I just came out for a walk.

DAVID

And a very long one, too, by the look of you. So why are you still here?

DONNA

It's a free country.

DAVID

(standing up and going over to her) There's nothing to be afraid of. You've heard everyone else.

DONNA

I wish you'd just leave me alone.

DAVID

Well, we're all staying here for a bit, so if you want to be alone, the path down's over there.

(DONNA doesn't move.)

DAVID

I didn't think so.

(For a moment there is silence.)

DAVID

This isn't turning into much of a party.

SHEILA

I wish you wouldn't joke about it. This is very serious for us.

DAVID

It's very serious for all of us. I don't think any of us are here for fun. I'm just trying to keep things light.

SHEILA

Well, don't.

ROSS

Have you seen it, er, David?

SHEILA

Ross....

DAVID

I don't know that now's a good time to talk about me, Ross.

JACK

Well, you seem to know about us.

DAVID

And let's leave it at that for now. I want to give young Ross here a few minutes to think, but maybe you could tell us what you saw, Jack.

JACK

You know most of it. We'd actually gone over the brow of the hill and were on our way back down the other side. We'd just stopped for coffee and I realised I'd left my flask behind. So I went back. I told them I'd catch them up, but, well, when I went back to the top of the hill, it was there. The light. I've never seen anything like it.

DAVID

Try and describe it.

JACK

It was incredible. It didn't look like it had any form or shape at first, but if you stared at it, there was something in the light. An oval. I watched it for, I don't know, maybe five minutes before I called the others. By the time they got there, Terry was first; it was flying off.

DAVID

So they only saw it move.

JACK

They all said it was a shooting star.

MARION

And wasn't it?

JACK

No! They only saw the last bit. I saw it.

DAVID

Marion, if you don't mind, I'd like to come back to what you feel about it in a minute. Is that all right?

MARION

I'm not sure what my feelings have got to do with anything, but yes, all right.

DAVID

Ross, are you ready to tell us? Only I think our friend Donna needs a little more time.

DONNA

I haven't seen anything. Don't you listen?

DAVID

Quite. Ross?

SHEILA

Ross reads too much science fiction.

DAVID

We'll hear about that in a minute. Ross?

ROSS

I know what Mum thinks, but I know what I saw. We only live over there (*He points*) and I was looking out of my bedroom window because I like looking at the stars. It was there. Hovering over the hill. I had to go, you know? Mum was in the living room *(he pauses, as if he was going to say something else and changed his mind)* -watching the telly, so I slipped out. I ran up the hill. I couldn't take my eyes off it. I stood on the top of the hill, watching it for ages. Then it flew off. *(He sounds incredibly sad at this memory)* I waited for it to come back, but it didn't.

DAVID

What did it look like?

ROSS

Like he said....

JACK

Jack.

ROSS

(With a slight smile) Like Jack said. It was sort of oval and very bright.

SHEILA

I found him wandering on the hill. I was scared stupid when I found he wasn't in his room. Then this nonsense about UFOs....

DAVID

Ross talks nonsense. Jack talks nonsense. Come on, Donna, why don't you talk nonsense too?

DONNA

How do you know my name?

DAVID

How do I know anything? You're Donna Warren nee Peel; otherwise, you wouldn't be here.

DONNA

All right. I saw it. It was bright and oval, and I saw it. Is that what you want to hear?

DAVID

Only if it's the truth, but it's only half the truth. You've all only told half the truth. I'm just going for a walk, then we'll have the other half.

JACK

Where are you going?

DAVID

Please. Not with ladies present.

JACK

Oh. Sorry.

DAVID

I won't be long. It'll be here soon and there's lots to talk about before then.

Blackout

SCENE TWO

(The same. When the lights come back up, a short time has elapsed. MARION is sitting huddled in her coat a few feet away from JACK, and ROSS is sitting nearer to DONNA than he is to SHEILA. DAVID has not returned.)

JACK

...the Brecon Beacons is a terrific walk, too. Takes a bit of stamina, but worth it.

MARION

All right, Jack. I think that's enough of the guided tour of Britain's walks, don't you think?

JACK

Sorry. I was just trying to fill in a bit of time until our friend gets back.

SHEILA

I don't think he is coming back. He's been a long time. Who is he, anyway?

JACK

I don't know. He just turned up. Mind you, you often meet some funny people when you're walking. I remember one time....

MARION

Jack, just shut up about walking, will you? No one wants to hear it. I certainly don't.

JACK

I thought you liked it.

MARION

I do. But there's only a certain number of times you can hear about it or see the slides. There's more to life than hiking, you know.

JACK

You never said.

MARION

You never asked. *(To SHEILA)* We met through the hiking club. We were both at an age when we thought we weren't going to meet anyone. I'm not sure if I actually married Jack or the whole club.

JACK

What's got into you, Marion? You've never said anything like this before.

MARION

I didn't know if you'd understand. I love you, Jack. You know that. And I like hiking. But not all the time. I'd like a romantic weekend in Paris sometimes, but I get Snowdonia.

JACK

What's brought this on?

MARION

Oh, I don't know. I've wanted to say it for ages.

JACK

Don't you think it would be better to wait until we get home?

MARION

I probably won't want to say it there. You know that night? The night of the walk up here? I wasn't ill. I just didn't want to go.

JACK

You only had to say.

MARION

No. You'd have talked me into it. And you saw a UFO on your own. We've never done anything on our own. Nothing. Not in six years. It must have been an incredible moment and I missed it.

JACK

(*sulky*) And whose fault was that?

MARION

I know! And all the time you've spent talking about it and the number of times I've heard you say, "It's a pity Marion missed it". The rest of the club still think it was a shooting star, you know. They laugh at you, Jack, you know that?

(*Pause.*)

JACK

Yes. I know.

MARION

That's why I came with you tonight. I want to see it with you this time. I want to share it. Then they can laugh at both of us.

DONNA

Isn't that lovely?

JACK

There's no need for that.

DONNA

Isn't there? Come on – Sheila, is it? - Why are you up here with Ross? Where's his dad? Why don't you and I talk about love and marriage?

SHEILA

I'd rather not.

DONNA

Suit yourself. I was married for eight months.

ROSS

What happened?

SHEILA

Ross, don't encourage her.

DONNA

We shared things. He shared his fists with me. We had nights of togetherness in the A&E. Then I didn't want to share anything with him and left. I ran out one night with nowhere to go and found myself up here. I saw a UFO and never went back.

ROSS

Because of the UFO?

DONNA

Sort of. It was beautiful. I stood there in its light, like a spotlight, and it was peaceful. I felt calm for the first time in eight months. I swear, even the bruises were better when it had gone.

JACK

They can't have been.

DONNA

Well, of course, they weren't. But they felt better. I felt better. So I went back, grabbed a bag and a black eye into the bargain and left. I stayed with a friend that night and got on a train to my sister's in Derby the next day. That was the longest night of my life.

SHEILA

Why?

DONNA

Well, Mike came after me, didn't he? He guessed which friend I'd gone to. It wasn't hard - he didn't let me have many. So he was there, knocking on the door, shouting, crying, pleading even. I got away the next day because Ann - that's my friend - called the police. I went to Derby and never saw him again.

SHEILA

Didn't he come after you there?

DONNA

No. He never bothered. I didn't think it would hurt me, but it did. But if he asked me to come back, I probably would have done. That was a year ago. I've hitched from Derby to come here and see if it'll come back. I need to see it again.

MARION

Why?

DONNA

I'm hoping it'll take me with it.

JACK

Oh, come on! Seriously?

DONNA

You can dream, can't you?

SHEILA

My husband died.

ROSS

You don't have to, Mum....

SHEILA

No. I want them to understand. It was a car crash. Ross was seven. It hasn't been easy bringing him up. He's very intelligent.

ROSS

Mum...

SHEILA

I don't see why you have to try and hide it, son. You should be proud.

ROSS

I don't.

SHEILA

You do. You always try and protect me, but I want you to be you, not your father. Ross has always had a vivid imagination. He used to write the most wonderful stories.

ROSS

I didn't imagine this! I saw it!

SHEILA

But it's the sort of thing you've always wanted to happen to you. That's what Dr. Theakston says.

ROSS

I never wanted to see him.

SHEILA

It was for the best. I thought you were having a breakdown of some kind.

ROSS

I wanted to talk to you, not him! But you were too... busy.

SHEILA

No, I wasn't.

ROSS

You weren't watching the telly that night. The telly was on, but you weren't watching it. You were drunk. You were out cold.

JACK

Ross, that isn't very nice.

SHEILA

It's true, though. It doesn't happen very often, but sometimes... I'm sorry, Ross. I sent you to Dr. Theakston because I couldn't cope.

ROSS

Dr. Theakston asked me once if I wanted aliens to be my dad. I don't think he's very good, Mum.

SHEILA

Of course, he is. That's what I pay him for.

JACK

Wait a minute. Is this Terry Theakston?

SHEILA

Yes, I think so. Do you know him?

JACK

He's in the hiking club.

MARION

(*quietly*) He's an idiot.

JACK

But he was there that night. He was the first up the hill. He saw it too. He said it was a shooting star, like the others, but I'm sure he saw it.

(*DAVID has reappeared unnoticed during this last line.*)

DAVID

And there you have it. Poor Ross has been treated, for want of a better word, by a man who can't believe his own eyes. Terry Theakston is one of the ones who laugh at Jack the most, isn't he, Marion?

MARION

You were listening.

DAVID

Put it this way, I wasn't far away. He is, though, isn't he?

MARION

He never shuts up about it.

DAVID

(*gesturing off*) And ladies and gentlemen, he's here tonight!

(They all look.)

DAVID

Only kidding. You didn't honestly think he would be, did you? No, tonight is for true believers only.

DONNA

Like you?

DAVID

If you like.

DONNA

Have you seen it too? You have, haven't you?

DAVID

Let's just say I've always had a healthy interest in the possibility of life on other planets.

JACK

Do you think there is?

DAVID

Do you?

JACK

How else would you explain what we saw?

DAVID

Weather balloon. Freak weather conditions. Shooting star.

JACK

It wasn't any of those.

ROSS

No. We all saw the same thing.

DAVID

You wouldn't believe what people used to say about the Northern Lights. Now, of course, there's no great mystery.

DONNA

So you're saying that we didn't see a UFO

DAVID

Not necessarily. But there are plenty of people who would.

ROSS

Is there a cover-up?

DAVID

That's not for me to say.

MARION

You seem to be the expert.

DAVID

Sit down a minute, all of you. Come on, Ross, I bet you like a good conspiracy theory. The X-Files and all that.

(*They all sit.*)

DAVID

What would happen, do you think, if we found out, and I mean found out for certain, that we are not alone? That there is intelligent life out there?

JACK

I don't know. It would be exciting.

DAVID

To you and me, perhaps. But what about the governments? There are some who would say they already know, but won't tell us.

SHEILA

Why? Haven't we got a right to know?

DAVID

Sure. But when, exactly, have any governments told you the things you have a right to know? Stop and think for a moment. What if the governments of this world knew for an absolute fact that planet Earth is not alone in supporting intelligent life? What if there's loads of life out there and they know it? Wouldn't it make this planet so much smaller? They'd have to admit for once that it's one planet, not a lot of separate nations. No need for wars anymore, no more need to ignore the fact that we need to look after each other. A lot of politicians wouldn't like that.

DONNA

Oh, come on! Nobody really wants war!

DAVID

You think? There's a lot of money to be made in the arms trade. Countries sell weapons to each other all the time, regardless of whether they're selling to allies or enemies. And there's nothing like a good war to make you feel patriotic. That usually helps the government of the day. How many elections have been won by war?

JACK

If that's true....

DAVID

I'm not saying it is. I'm just saying, "What if?" I think you'll agree it makes sense, though. But you're here for more personal reasons, aren't you? Jack, you came to see it again and Marion wants to share it. Ross is here because his life hasn't made much sense so far and he wants something to hold onto, while Sheila wants to make sense of Ross. And Donna... Donna's looking for an escape. Well, it should be here soon, and I hope you all find what you're looking for, really I do. But I'm not sure you will.

DONNA

You think you know everything, don't you?

DAVID

Not everything, but no one's perfect.

JACK

You've got no business knowing anything about us. *(Advances on DAVID)* I don't want someone knowing this much about me. I mean, who are you? What right have you got to spy on us?

DAVID

Steady on, Jack. No one's spying on you. Most of the information I've got is guesswork. The rest is stuff you've told me or each other. No one made you talk.

DONNA

You tricked us.

DAVID

No trick. I think you wanted to talk. All of you.

JACK

Well, don't just stop there. What now? Come on. You're the one with all the answers.

DAVID

I don't have any answers. You've got to find them out for yourselves.

JACK

That's a cop-out. Where? Where do we look?

DAVID

You already know the answer to that one.

JACK

How do you mean?

DAVID

It's not for me to say. But try looking a little closer to home.

DONNA

I don't understand.

DAVID

Look at it like this...you'd already walked out on your husband before you saw the UFO.

DONNA

But I'd have gone back....

DAVID

Would you? Well, I suppose we'll never know, will we?

JACK

Oh, there's something you don't know, is there?

DAVID

There are plenty of things I don't know. What I do know is that you've all talked to each other tonight, probably more than you've talked for a long time. And all because of a UFO that some of you haven't even seen. Odd that, isn't it?

SHEILA

No. It was because of you.

DAVID

I wasn't even here for the best bit. If it hadn't been for the UFO, you wouldn't have come here. If you hadn't come here, you wouldn't have talked.

JACK

If it hadn't been for that bloody UFO, we wouldn't have had anything to talk about.

DAVID

Really? Are you taking Marion to Paris, then?

JACK

Damn right. First booking I can get.

MARION

(Hugging him) Oh, Jack!

DAVID

Need I say more?

JACK

In fact, I think we should go home now and see if we can arrange a date.

MARION

But what about the UFO?

JACK

I've seen it. It's only a light in the sky. (To DAVID) Thank you.

DAVID

You've changed your tune. A minute ago, you wanted to kill me.

JACK

Sorry about that. I think I was missing the point. Thanks anyway. Goodnight everyone.

(JACK and MARION gather their things together and exit arm in arm. As they go, we hear their voices trailing off.)

JACK

(off) We can't go the weekend of the 14th, though, it's the AGM....

MARION

(off) Sod the AGM.

(There is a pause.)

SHEILA

Ross, I think we'd better go, too.

ROSS

I thought you wanted to see it.

SHEILA

I don't need to see it. You can tell me.

ROSS

But you've got to see it. You won't believe me if you don't.

SHEILA

Does that matter? You believe it. That's enough. Anyway, if it comes, we'll see it from your bedroom window, won't we?

(Oblivious to anyone else, they walk off.)

SHEILA

(As they go) Look, isn't that the Plough?

ROSS

(off) Mum! It's Orion. That's the Plough.

(Another pause.)

DAVID

They'll be all right. Given time. *(To DONNA)* Are you going too?

DONNA

No. I want to see it.

DAVID

What for? Are you still hoping they'll take you away from all this?

DONNA

No. I didn't really think they would.

DAVID

Then why?

DONNA

Just because. I need to know it was real.

DAVID

What if it wasn't? What if it doesn't come tonight?

DONNA

It's got to! I've got nothing else.

DAVID

Go back to your family, Donna. Get a divorce. Then get on with your life. Oh, and get a shower while you're at it.

DONNA

(smiles) What about you?

DAVID

Me?

DONNA

We never did hear about you.

DAVID

There's not much to tell. I'm going home myself in a minute.

DONNA

Are you?

DAVID

Go home, Donna.

DONNA

Will I see you again?

DAVID

I don't get to Derby much. But keep watching the skies, Donna. Anything can happen.

DONNA

Well, 'bye then.

DAVID

How will you get home?

DONNA

I'll find somewhere for the night. Then get the train in the morning.

DAVID

Twenty-four, Greenway.

DONNA

Sorry?

DAVID

Twenty-four, Greenway. Sheila's house. It's worth a try. She might be glad of the company.

DONNA

Thanks. 'Bye.

DAVID

Goodbye, Donna. Good luck.

(*DONNA exits. DAVID watches her go, then wanders to the front of the stage. He looks up into the sky. After a second or two, the lights begin to get gradually brighter and DAVID smiles. Before the lights reach their peak...*)

CURTAIN

Night of the Long Beards

A One Act Comedy

CAST IN ORDER OF APPEARANCE

ALBERT FORBES

HELEN ELLISON

ALICIA WINTERS

BILLY KING

GINNY BELMONT

STEVE

The scene is the storeroom of a large department store.

The time is the present day, getting on for Christmas.

SCENE ONE

The scene is a storeroom of a large department store. Apart from a selection of packing cases scattered around, there are also several chairs and a coat stand. The whole room is organised chaos but without the organisation. As we will learn, the room is being used as a staff room for the staff of the store's Christmas grotto.

As the curtain opens, ALBERT FORBES, a rather morose man in his fifties/sixties, is sitting on one of the chairs. He is drinking what appears to be a cup of coffee. After a couple of sips, he glances around, then takes a hip flask out of his pocket and pours some of its contents into the coffee and tries it again. This seems to make it taste better.

Behind him, he hears the door open and replaces the flask in his pocket. HELEN ELLISON enters. She is in her late forties and carries a suitcase.

HELEN

Morning, Albert. Back again this year?

ALBERT

Back again every year. I just can't stay away. I thought they'd have pensioned you off, though.

HELEN

I did think about it, but I thought, well, one more year.

ALBERT

How many years have I heard that?

HELEN

Who's the other Santa this year? Billy?

ALBERT

Billy is second Santa. I'm Head Santa this year.

HELEN

You've had a promotion? Congratulations.

ALBERT

Of course, it's not official yet. That's why I got here early. I'll have a word with old Mrs.Whitlock from Personnel. They've got to recognise seniority.

HELEN

It's called Human Resources now.

ALBERT

What is?

HELEN

Personnel. It's called Human Resources.

ALBERT

That's a stupid thing to call it. It sounds like bodily functions.

HELEN

Don't be crude. Anyway, I heard there's a new Human Resources Manager this year.

ALBERT

Mrs.Whitlock finally got the push?

HELEN

Retired. She is seventy-four, Albert.

ALBERT

Don't tell me she's going to be an elf this year.

HELEN

There's no need for that.

ALBERT

Speaking of which, any idea who else is elfing this year?

HELEN

I saw Ginny coming in.

ALBERT

Oh, God. She's hopeless.

HELEN

She's good with the kids.

ALBERT

She can relate to them. She's still one herself.

HELEN

She must be forty-ish now.

ALBERT

Doesn't stop her.

(The door opens, and ALICIA WINTERS, the new Human Resources Manager, enters. She is in her twenties, power-dressed and anxious to appear efficient. Her main problem is that her college business studies course has not really prepared her to work with people. She consults a large ring file as she surveys the room.)

ALICIA

Ah. Good. You're here. And you would be Mr. King?

ALBERT

No.

ALICIA

Excellent. I'm Ms. Winters, the new...Sorry, did you say 'no'?

ALBERT

Yes.

ALICIA

You said 'yes'?

ALBERT

No, yes, I said 'no'.

ALICIA

Can we start this again?

ALBERT

Yes. No, I'm not Mr. King. I'm Mr. Forbes.

ALICIA

Oh.

ALBERT

Albert Forbes. Head Santa.

ALICIA

I understood Mr. King was Head Santa.

ALBERT

Sit down. There are things you ought to know. *(ALICIA obediently sits)* Billy, that's Mr. King, tries this on every year. It used to work with Mrs. Whitlock because her memory was going, and she never wrote anything down. Every year Billy got here first, told Old Whitlock he was Head Santa and she believed him.

ALICIA

Why would she do that?

ALBERT

Because it worked.

ALICIA

So why didn't you get here first?

ALBERT

I have now, haven't I?

ALICIA

Well, as I understand it, Head Santa is only an honorary title.

ALBERT

Honorary title? It's not a title, it's a principle. I've been doing Santa in this store for fifteen years now. I worked with Chris Cringle, one of the greatest Santas of all time.

ALICIA

Chris Cringle?

HELEN

(Who has been watching with interest) It wasn't his real name. His real name was Chris Higginbottom. I'm Helen Ellison, by the way.

ALICIA

Pleased to meet you.

HELEN

Likewise.

ALBERT

Anyway, that little upstart's only been Santaing for seven years. He said it was only a stopgap while he was resting between acting jobs. He's been resting ever since.

(At this point, the door opens, and BILLY KING enters. He is younger than ALBERT but rather more flamboyant.)

BILLY

Oh, hello, Albert, Helen. Back again, are we? And you must be Ms. Winters. I've heard so much about you. *(He kisses ALICIA's hand)*

ALICIA

(startled) Oh!

BILLY

Albert, are you still driving that dreadful old Mini?

ALBERT

Why?

BILLY

It's being clamped.

ALBERT

Oh bugger. Not again. *(He hurries out)*

BILLY

He'll never learn. Now then, Ms. Winters, I take it you want me to be Head Santa again this year.

ALICIA

Oh, well, Mr.-er-Forbes has just told me that he was Head Santa.

BILLY

He tries that every year. Used to turn up early and try and convince old Mrs.Whitlock that she'd promised it to him. Rather naughty of him, really, considering Mrs.W's memory was going and she never wrote anything down.

ALICIA

That's what he said about you.

BILLY

Did he? But there's nothing wrong with my memory.

ALICIA

No, he said....

HELEN

He's playing with you, dear.

ALICIA

(flustered) Anyway, as I was explaining to Mr. Forbes, Head Santa is really only an honorary title.

BILLY

Oh, dear. You have got a lot to learn. It isn't honorary; it's the greatest honour. And I'm afraid poor Albert really isn't up to it.

ALICIA

Really? Why not?

BILLY

Well, I don't like to gossip, but... *(he mimes drinking. ALICIA looks blank)* You know, he... *(mimes drinking again but with rather more gusto. Still nothing.)* Oh, for God's sake, dear, he's a drinker.

ALICIA

Is he? *(She looks to HELEN for confirmation)*

HELEN

I'm afraid he does like a drink, yes, but....

ALICIA

We can't have a drunken Santa!

HELEN

Well, he doesn't exactly....

BILLY

You're absolutely right. Mrs.Whitlock didn't understand, of course, but she was usually three sheets to the wind herself.

HELEN

(warning) Billy....

BILLY

And his temper... Well, what can I say? I'd bet that any second now, he'll come storming through that door. I know the signs.

(And, of course, at that moment, ALBERT comes storming through the door.)

ALBERT

I want a word with you, Billy King.

BILLY

Told you.

ALBERT

My car wasn't being clamped!

BILLY

Wasn't it? Oh, I'm terribly sorry old man, I could have sworn ....

ALBERT

It was just a ploy!

BILLY

Now really ....

ALBERT

I bet you did that so you'd get Head Santa. He did, didn't he, Helen?

HELEN

Leave me out of this.

ALICIA

Mr. Forbes ...

ALBERT

I don't know what he's been telling you, but ...

ALICIA

Mr. Forbes ...

ALBERT

He lies, you know. Habitually.

BILLY

That's rich coming from you.

ALBERT

He calls himself an actor ...

BILLY

I worked with stars of "Coronation Street".

ALBERT

They were in panto. You were half a cow.

BILLY

That isn't the point.

ALBERT

You were the back end. You didn't even moo.

ALICIA

Gentlemen, please ...

BILLY

I've worked in rep.

ALBERT

You were a callboy in 1971!

ALICIA

(*yelling at the top of her voice*) GENTLEMEN PLEASE!!

(*There is a stunned silence.*)

ALICIA

Sorry.

HELEN

Don't apologise. I've been dying to do that for years.

ALICIA

I think we'll all agree that our object is to provide the best grotto in this city, and arguing amongst ourselves will not help. Now Head Office has told me that this grotto needs updating, so to that end, this year will see the introduction of a few changes, including (consults her file) the Chrismatic Automated Snowman, which I'm sure you'll find very impressive ...

ALBERT

The what?

ALICIA

Chrismatic Automated Snowman. It's, well, it's a kind of ...

ALBERT

Automated Snowman. I thought so. I just wanted to see if you could say it twice. Why do we need one?

ALICIA

This is the twenty-first century, Mr. Forbes.

BILLY

What's next? Robot Santas? Electric Elves?

ALICIA

Next year, maybe. Now as I was saying ...

HELEN

What did you say?

ALICIA

I said, "as I was saying ..."

HELEN

Before that. You said, "Next year". What, Electric Elves?

ALICIA

It's an option we're looking at, yes. Children expect these things.

HELEN

Why don't you do away with the children as well? If the grotto's going to be fake, let's make everything fake, shall we?

ALICIA

I think we're missing the point.

HELEN

I don't think we are. You certainly are.

ALICIA

I'm sorry you feel like that, but if you'll excuse me, the snowman's due.

(She exits. There is a pause.)

HELEN

Something's got to be done.

ALBERT

Like what?

HELEN

I'm not sure. But if we don't do something, we'll all be out of a job.

BILLY

I see what you mean. Look, let's spread the word. Get everyone here early tomorrow. We'll have a meeting before she gets here. It's down to us the save Christmas.

(Pause)

ALBERT

That was a bit dramatic, wasn't it?

BILLY

Sorry.

Blackout

SCENE TWO

The same. The next morning. BILLY is sitting at a table with a sheaf of papers in front of him. GINNY

BELMONT enters. She is in her forties and, as previously hinted, rather over-excitable. BILLY does not notice her enter until she hurls the holdall she is carrying into a corner and shouts "BACK OF THE NET!" This makes BILLY jump up, scattering his papers.

BILLY

Ginny, do you mind?

GINNY

Oh, sorry, Billy. I didn't know you were here.

BILLY

(starting to gather his papers together) So I gathered.

GINNY

(rushing over) Can I help?

BILLY

You've already done more than enough, Ginny.

GINNY

(pouting) No one ever lets me help.

BILLY

I wonder why.

GINNY

(picking up a newspaper off the floor) Here's one!

BILLY

That's a newspaper.

GINNY

Not yours, then.

BILLY

Not mine. Look, Ginny, there's something you can do to help. *(He puts his arm around her shoulder and leads her to a chair on the far side of the room)* You can sit here.

GINNY

(eager to please) Now what?

BILLY

No, just sit there.

GINNY

How does that help?

BILLY

It helps me enormously.

(HELEN enters.)

HELEN

Albert's on his way.

GINNY

Morning, Helen.

HELEN

Morning, Ginny. What are you doing over there?

GINNY

Helping Billy.

HELEN

(slightly bemused) Oh, good. Where's everyone else?

BILLY

It's just us, I'm afraid. Apparently, the Job Centre didn't send any more elves this year.

HELEN

Why not?

BILLY

They only had two applications, I believe. One was from a retired truck driver; the other was from a redundant undertaker.

HELEN

Why would an undertaker be redundant?

BILLY

I didn't like to ask.

HELEN

What are you up to, Billy?

BILLY

I'm trying to work on a plan, my dear. It would be easier without the interruptions.

GINNY

What plan?

BILLY

Nothing which need concern you at the moment.

GINNY

There's something going on, isn't there? There was something going on all day yesterday and it's still going on today. I know.

HELEN

Well, good for you, Ginny. We'd better tell her, Billy.

BILLY

I don't see why.

HELEN

She's involved as any of us.

GINNY

I'm here.

BILLY

Yes, we know you are.

GINNY

Only you were talking about me like I'm not, but I am.

HELEN

Billy?

BILLY

Oh, very well. Basically, Ginny, the management, in their wisdom, has decided that they can do without old-fashioned grottos like ours and want to replace us all with robots.

GINNY

Robots?

BILLY

Robots.

GINNY

Where would they get a robot of me from?

BILLY

And I thought this would be easy. Never mind the details for now, Ginny dear, the point is that we have to stop them, or we're all out of a job.

GINNY

Then we'll have to be really good, won't we?

HELEN

Good?

GINNY

If we're really extra good, then they won't want to replace us, and everything will be all right.

BILLY

Of course! Why didn't I think of that?

GINNY

I don't know. It just came to me.

BILLY

Because it doesn't work like that! Progress has no interest in quality. It just lumbers on destroying everything in its path.

GINNY

Oooh, I'll bet you were really good at the RSC.

HELEN

(aside to BILLY) The RSC?

BILLY

(aside) The Roxy, Scunthorpe Company. I'll tell you some day.

(But not today, because the door opens and ALICIA enters. With her is a man in his thirties, whom we'll call STEVE, because that is his name.)

ALICIA

Oh good. You're all here early. Mr. Forbes not here yet?

BILLY

(to himself) Of all the mornings! *(To ALICIA)* No, Albert isn't here yet. He had some business to attend to.

ALICIA

Oh. I hope he isn't long. Punctuality is terribly important, I always feel.

BILLY

So do we. That's why we're here early.

GINNY

We're hatching.

ALICIA

Hatching?

GINNY

A plot!

(This exchange is interrupted by STEVE noisily clearing his throat.)

ALICIA

Oh, I'm sorry. Everybody, this is Steve. Steve is from ChrisCo. and he'll be responsible for installing and maintaining the Snowman.

STEVE

Hi.

BILLY

ChrisCo. Lord help us, whatever next?

GINNY

I'm Ginny. This is Helen and Billy.

STEVE

Hi. Is there anywhere I can get a coffee?

BILLY

There's a coffee machine down the corridor. You'll like it, it isn't human.

STEVE

Hey. listen Bill, there's no need for bad vibes, man. I'm just here to do a job.

BILLY

So are we, 'man'.

ALICIA

Good. Well, now we're all acquainted, I'll be in my office if anyone needs me.

(She exits.)

BILLY

If anyone ....

HELEN

Ssh! Ginny, why don't you show Steve here where the coffee machine is?

GINNY

Okay. Come on, Steve.

STEVE

Oh, right. (*He follows her out*)

BILLY

What was that for?

HELEN

I've had an idea, but for it to work, we've got to be polite to Steve.

BILLY

Why? So, we don't upset his 'vibes'?

HELEN

No, because he knows how the Snowman works.

BILLY

I'm not sure I want to know how ....

HELEN

If we don't know how it works, we can't sabotage it, can we?

BILLY

Helen, you're evil!

HELEN

Aren't I just?

(ALBERT enters. He is obviously furious.)

HELEN

Morning, Albert.

ALBERT

Mmph.

HELEN

What's the matter, Albert? You don't seem your usual cheery self this morning.

ALBERT

The world is full of idiots.

BILLY

We know that.

ALBERT

Do you know where I've just been?

HELEN

Oddly enough, no.

ALBERT

I've been to the Citizens Advice Bureau. I was after some advice on Unfair Dismissal.

HELEN

What did they say?

ALBERT

Well, I told them that I was in danger of not being Santa anymore because of a robot and they gave me a lecture on how Santa doesn't really exist and recommended a doctor to help with my robot problem. I don't think they were taking me seriously.

HELEN

Why not?

ALBERT

They recommended Doctor Who.

HELEN

Never mind. We've come up with a plan. Now you won't like it at first because it means you'll have to be nice to someone you won't want to be nice to.

ALBERT

What, Ginny?

(GINNY and STEVE enter. STEVE is carrying a cup of coffee.)

GINNY

What Ginny what?

BILLY

That was a classic mangling of the English language, even by your standards.

GINNY

What?

HELEN

Never mind. Steve, this is Albert Forbes, our other Santa. Steve is going to install our nice new Snowman.

ALBERT

He's what?... He's...he's the one? ... Him? ... And you want me to ... him?... Nice? Nice? What do you mean by... HIM?!

HELEN

Yes, Albert. Steve's the one we mentioned to you.

STEVE

I'm glad you understood that. Hi Al.

ALBERT

Hmph.

BILLY

Now, Albert. Steve's just doing a job like anyone else. You don't want to give him bad vibes *(to STEVE)*, isn't that right, man?

STEVE

Are you taking the piss?

HELEN

We were only just saying, Steve, we're fascinated by this Snowman, aren't we, Billy?

BILLY

Fascinated.

STEVE

Are you?

HELEN

We'd be very interested in knowing how it works.

STEVE

Do you want me to show you?

HELEN

We'd love you to, wouldn't we, Billy?

BILLY

Love it.

STEVE

Well, come on. I'll show you as I install it.

HELEN

Smashing.

BILLY

Lovely.

(They exit.

A pause.)

ALBERT

That's it! They've gone stark raving mad. If they've defected to the other side, it's all down to me now.

GINNY

What about me?

ALBERT

I think that's what I said. (*An idea suddenly strikes him*) This could work out perfectly! If Billy's on their side, I could bring them all down at once. By the time this is all over, there's only be one Santa left in this place! (*He exits hurriedly*)

GINNY

Is it just me, or this turning out to be a strange day?

Blackout

SCENE THREE

(The next morning.

ALICIA is sitting on one of the chairs. She checks her watch and sighs. She is just about to get up and leave, when ALBERT enters.)

ALICIA

Ah. There you are.

ALBERT

Sorry. I was trying to find a parking space.

ALICIA

I was about to go back to my office.

ALBERT

I won't keep you long -er- Alicia. But there's something I think you ought to know. Nice snowman, by the way.

ALICIA

Oh, you like it?

ALBERT

Very effective. I must admit I never get tired of hearing "Frosty The Snowman" over and -er- over again.

ALICIA

Do you think it's a bit repetitive?

ALBERT

Well ...

ALICIA

Don't be afraid of speaking your mind, Albert. We all have to work together and I value your input.

ALBERT

It is a bit repetitive. Particularly if you work here.

ALICIA

Well, that's easily solved. It's only on a disc. You can get other discs, you know. They do "Winter Wonderland" and "We Wish You A Merry Christmas" as well.

ALBERT

(not entirely convinced) Lovely.

ALICIA

Three songs should provide enough variety, shouldn't they?

ALBERT

If they must.

ALICIA

Now then. What was it you wanted to talk to me about?

ALBERT

Well, it's a bit delicate.

ALICIA

You can tell me.

ALBERT

It's a bit difficult. I haven't known you very long.

ALICIA

Don't worry about that, Albert.

ALBERT

You see, there's this person I know. He's always felt things very strongly but tried to hide it.

ALICIA

I think we've all done that.

ALBERT

Quite. But this person has let his feelings get the better of him this time. I've -er- heard things which make me think he's really gone off the deep end. I think he's desperate.

ALICIA

Desperate? Really?

ALBERT

He could do anything.

ALICIA

Oh, crikey!

ALBERT

"Crikey"? Do people still say that?

ALICIA

I do. I don't like swearing. Carry on.

ALBERT

Well ... this person feels so strongly about this ... issue that anything could happen.

ALICIA

I see. It's very good of you to tell me, Albert. I know it must have been very hard for you. But you don't need to pretend any more. It's best if everything's out in the open. It's you, isn't it?

ALBERT

What is?

ALICIA

This person.

ALBERT

What? No!

ALICIA

No?

ALBERT

It's Billy.

ALICIA

Billy?

ALBERT

I tried to tell you.

ALICIA

I see. *(She gets up)* Oh, dear. I was afraid something like this might happen. Why do I always end up working with single men? I can't help the way I look.

ALBERT

The way you look? What's that got to do with anything?

ALICIA

I would have thought that was obvious. I'm sorry, Albert. I must catch Billy as he comes in. He needs to know I can't return his affection before this gets any further. Thank you, Albert.

(She exits, leaving ALBERT to realise the horrible truth.)

ALBERT

(*Running to the door*) You've got it all wrong! He doesn't fancy you! He wants to kill your snowman! (*He is too late. She has gone.*) Oh crikey. (*He sinks down into a chair*)

(GINNY enters. As usual, she throws her holdall into the corner and shouts "BACK OF THE NET!")

ALBERT

Ginny, do that one more time and that won't be the only old bag that gets thrown across the room.

GINNY

Not having a good morning, Albert?

ALBERT

Not really. I tried to tell that silly Winters woman that Billy wants to sabotage her snowman so she'd sack him and make me Head Santa, but she thinks he fancies her instead.

GINNY

That's a bit of a mess, isn't it?

ALBERT

Yes, it is.

GINNY

I didn't know Billy fancied Ms. Winters.

ALBERT

He doesn't. He ... oh, why do I even bother?

GINNY

So what are you going to do?

ALBERT

I don't know. Billy will set her straight about fancying her, I hope. But the snowman...I think I need to find out what they're planning.

GINNY

(not really paying attention) It's funny. Billy never really struck me as the romantic type.

ALBERT

Billy? But he isn't.

GINNY

I've been trying to get him to notice me for years. That's typical that is. As soon as a younger, pretty girl comes along ...

ALBERT

Weren't you listening? He doesn't fancy Alicia!

GINNY

Then who does he fancy?

ALBERT

No one. I don't know. It could even be you, for all I know.

GINNY

Really?

ALBERT

Oh, this is hopeless. I'm going to have to sort all this out myself. Just wait here, Ginny.

GINNY

Yes. Billy might come back.

(ALBERT rolls his eyes heavenwards and exits. GINNY goes over to her holdall and roots around in it, taking out a make-up bag. She sits on a chair and examines her make-up in a hand mirror. BILLY and HELEN enter.)

BILLY

... and I tell you, Helen, it was probably the most bizarre conversation I've ever had.

HELEN

You don't think the strain's getting to her already, do you?

BILLY

It sounds like it. Ginny, have you seen Alicia today?

GINNY

(*coldly*) No. Why?

BILLY

I just wondered if she'd seemed strange to you.

GINNY

No stranger than usual.

BILLY

She's just collared me and told me she was letting me down gently and that staff relationships just weren't on. I don't know what made her think I was interested. She's only a kid.

GINNY

(*suddenly becoming a little more coy*) Why? Do you prefer more mature women, Billy?

BILLY

I suppose so ... If I had to. Probably. Yes.

GINNY

(*looking at her watch*) It's time we were getting ready.

BILLY

Oh Lord, yes.

GINNY

Don't worry, Billy. I'm going to be the best little elf you've ever had.

BILLY

That conjures up a variety of images, most of which are unrepeatable in mixed company.

GINNY

I'll see you later, Billy.

BILLY

I know. I can't really see how it can be avoided.

(BILLY exits, almost colliding with STEVE.)

STEVE

He's in a hurry.

GINNY

He's playing hard to get.

HELEN

Very hard.

STEVE

The snowman seems to be working okay. The kids love it.

HELEN

It's surprisingly straightforward, isn't it? I mean, you'd think there'd be more to it than just sticking a disc in the back of its head. You'd think it would have Bluetooth or something.

STEVE

Well, the movements are a bit more complicated. There's a lot of technology involved there.

HELEN

But the music's just a disc.

STEVE

Yes. I mean future models might be Wi-Fi, but at the moment, yes.

GINNY

Could I have a word, please, Helen?

HELEN

Oh, yes. Sure.

STEVE

I'll just be over -er- here.

(He wanders off.)

GINNY

Helen....

HELEN

Ginny.

GINNY

... just imagine if, well, if you were interested in someone.

HELEN

Someone?

GINNY

Someone of the opposite -er- sort of sex thing. Have you?

HELEN

Have I what?

GINNY

Ever been interested?

HELEN

I married one.

GINNY

Oh yes. So you did. But what if you were and they weren't?

HELEN

I'm losing track. Weren't what?

GINNY

Interested.

HELEN

I probably wouldn't have married him.

GINNY

No, I mean hypo-thingy.

HELEN -Dermic?

GINNY -Thetically. If you were interested in them and they weren't interested in you, what would you do?

HELEN

I really don't know. It's been a hell of a long time since I did anything like that.

STEVE

Music.

GINNY

Sorry?

STEVE

Music usually helps. Or, well, it does for me. Like, if I'm chatting someone up in the pub, I usually sneak off at some point and put something soppy on the jukebox. If she likes it, I tell her I put it on for her and I'm in there. If she doesn't, I've only wasted a quid.

HELEN

Well, thanks for that.

GINNY

No, wait. He might have a point.

HELEN

A point? Him?

STEVE

Oh thanks.

GINNY

Could you show me how the snowman works?

STEVE

The snowman? Why? Oh no. No chance. I want to keep my job.

HELEN

But you don't mind putting us out of ours.

STEVE

It's nothing personal. But you can't use the snowman just to serenade some bloke you fancy.

GINNY

It's not just any bloke. I want to serenade Santa.

HELEN

What, Albert?

GINNY

No! Billy! You've known him longer than me, Helen. What sort of music does he like?

HELEN

Oh, I'm not sure. *(Suddenly sensing an opportunity)* No, hang on. He once told me he like the Beach Boys.

GINNY

The Beach Boys? Billy? He doesn't seem the type.

HELEN

There's no accounting for taste.

GINNY

Helen, could you do me a favour?

HELEN

What's that?

GINNY

Could you do my shift for me? I've got to nip out to the record shop.

HELEN

Sure. No problem.

GINNY

Thanks. *(She exits)*

STEVE

Don't tell me she's going to … No. Sorry. I can't let her do that.

HELEN

Don't worry. She won't be able to figure out how to work it. Trust me.

STEVE

I don't trust any of you lot. *(Starts to go)*

HELEN

Where are you going?

STEVE

I'm going to guard my snowman.

(He exits.)

HELEN

Oh, Billy. I'm going to be the best little elf you've ever had.

Blackout

SCENE FOUR

(Later that day. ALBERT is sitting on one of the chairs. "Winter Wonderland" can be heard playing off. ALICIA enters.)

ALICIA

Oh. Isn't Steve here?

ALBERT

Steve?

ALICIA

Steve, the technician Steve.

ALBERT

Oh, that Steve. *(Looks carefully around)* No.

ALICIA

That's funny. Ginny said he was looking for me.

ALBERT

She was probably mistaken. Listen, while we're here, I want to clear something up.

ALICIA

Oh. That. Don't worry. I quite understand. I've spoken to Billy and set him straight.

ALBERT

No, I think, well ... I don't think I explained it very well. The thing is, and I don't like to speak ill of a colleague, but, and there's no easy way to say this, Billy wants to sabotage your snowman.

ALICIA

Billy?

ALBERT

Yes.

ALICIA

The snowman?

ALBERT

Yes.

ALICIA

But why? Just because I turned him down?

ALBERT

Oh, I don't know. Something about losing his job or something. Some people just don't like progress. I think Helen and Ginny are in on it too.

(STEVE enters.)

STEVE

There you are.

ALICIA

Yes?

STEVE

Someone said you wanted to see me. I don't know names.

ALICIA

But Ginny said you were looking for me.

STEVE

Ginny said? Is that her name?

(A pause.)

STEVE and ALICIA together

THE SNOWMAN!

(They rush off. As they do, "Surfin' USA" starts to blare out from off.)

ALBERT

I've got to see this.

(He exits. The music continues for a few moments, then cuts of abruptly. After a pause, during which raised voices can be heard offstage, "Winter Wonderland" can be heard resuming.

ALICIA storms back on, followed by STEVE.)

ALICIA

That's IT. They've been trying to undermine me from the start.

STEVE

Sorry. I tried to guard it.

ALICIA

I want to see them all in here now. Both Santas and those two bloody elves.

STEVE

I'll tell them, shall I?

ALICIA

You do that.

(STEVE exits. ALICIA paces furiously. HELEN and ALBERT enter.)

ALICIA

Where are they?

HELEN

Who?

ALICIA

Psycho Santa and his pointy eared sidekick.

HELEN

They're just getting changed.

ALBERT

I warned you, didn't I? Or at least I tried to.

ALICIA

Yes, I know you did. But would you have warned me if you hadn't wanted to be Head Santa?

ALBERT

Well, of course, I would.

ALICIA

Steve, how long would it take to get the Chrismatic Automated Santa and a couple of Cyber-elves?

STEVE

Couple of days, I suppose.

ALICIA

Get them here tomorrow.

STEVE

I'll do what I can.

ALICIA

If you can't, you'll be out of a job too.

HELEN

What are you doing?

ALICIA

Replacing you. All of you.

HELEN

You can't do that!

ALICIA

I can and I have.

(GINNY and BILLY enter.)

BILLY

Will this take long? I'm due on again soon.

ALICIA

Oh no, you're not. You're sacked, the lot of you.

GINNY

But why?

ALICIA

I would have thought that was obvious. You've been messing me around since I got here. Turning my snowman into a surfer was the last straw. Your robot replacements will be here tomorrow.

STEVE

Hopefully.

ALBERT

Is it just me, or has this started to sound like a cheap science fiction film?

GINNY

It's all my fault.

ALICIA

I wondered if it might be.

GINNY

I was only trying to get Billy to notice me.

BILLY

Ginny, I couldn't miss you ... wait a minute. What did you say?

GINNY

I wanted you to notice me. I couldn't think of any other way.

BILLY

Why would you want me to notice you? I work with you.

GINNY

Isn't it obvious?

ALBERT

Look, could you two put your love life on hold for a minute?

BILLY

Love life? I haven't got a ... Ginny?

ALBERT

Don't you get it? She's trying to sack us!

ALICIA

Not trying.

HELEN

You can't get rid of us from the grotto. It makes a bomb.

(As if on cue, there is a large explosion off. There is a pause.)

STEVE

I'll go, shall I?

(He exits. There is another pause. STEVE returns carrying the head of a snowman which is still smouldering, which he dumps on the floor.)

STEVE

Ladies and gentlemen, we have a bit of a problem with the snowman. Some kid poured a hot chocolate into it. It's the marshmallows that have done the damage.

ALBERT

The wonders of modern technology, eh? I just wash my costume when that happens.

HELEN

That's it, then. No grotto.

ALICIA

Unless ... *(she looks from one to another)*

BILLY

No. Sorry.

ALBERT

Can't do it.

HELEN

We're all sacked, remember?

GINNY

So there!

ALICIA

You can have your jobs back.

ALBERT

I'm not sure about that, are you, Billy?

BILLY

On that money? I don't think so, Albert.

HELEN

In any case, machines are so much more efficient.

ALICIA

Please?

(A pause.)

ALBERT

Did you just say please?

ALICIA

Yes!

BILLY

Things must be desperate.

ALICIA

They are!

ALBERT

I don't know. We'd have to talk terms.

ALICIA

Like what?

BILLY

A pay rise. Twenty per cent.

ALICIA

Ten.

BILLY

Fifteen.

ALICIA

Done.

ALBERT

No more robots.

ALICIA

Definitely not.

STEVE

Hang on, that means I'm out of a job.

HELEN

It's nothing personal. Hang on, what size are you?

STEVE

Size?

HELEN

Clothes size.

STEVE

Medium to large. Why?

HELEN

Congratulations, you're an elf.

STEVE

Now wait a minute ...!

GINNY

It's fun. You'll like it.

STEVE

Oh no, I won't.

(GINNY and HELEN drag STEVE to the back of the set and start to dress him in an elf costume.)

BILLY

There is one other thing.

ALICIA

Will it take long?

BILLY

Who's Head Santa?

ALICIA

Head Santa? At a time like this?

BILLY

It's important.

ALICIA

All right. Billy.

ALBERT

Billy?

ALICIA

And you're...you're Senior Santa.

ALBERT

(rather pleased) Senior Santa?

ALICIA

Yes! Now will you get on with it?

BILLY

Say please again.

ALICIA

Pretty please! Just do it!

BILLY

Right. Do you want this shift, Albert?

ALBERT

Well, as Senior Santa, I think I should. Besides, it'll give you more time with Ginny.

BILLY

No, it's okay. I'll do it.

(He exits hurriedly.)

GINNY

Wait a minute, Billy. I'll do this shift with you.

(She hurries after him.)

ALICIA

Nice costume, Steve. Suits you.

STEVE

Oh hell.

ALBERT

(exchanging a glance with HELEN) There is just one other condition for us going back to work, Alicia.

ALICIA

What's that?

HELEN

You join us. What are you, about a fourteen?

ALICIA

I'm a twelve! But ... oh no. No way. I'm head of Human Resources.

HELEN

And you're about to find out what it's like on the sharp end. After all, it would be a shame if your superiors found out about the amazing surfing exploding snowman.

ALICIA

You wouldn't!

HELEN

Oh yes, we would. Now come on. Get your ears on. And your little hat. It'll be a whole new you.

ALBERT

And don't worry. It'll soon be Christmas.

Blackout

CURTAIN

Afterword

(Including some notes on staging)

Looking back, it's hard to think now that these plays were written at what we must now call the turn of the century. In fact, the manuscript for Some of Us Are Looking at the Stars was actually written at the end of the last century, judging by the dates on which the UFO was supposed to have been sighted. This means that some things might be a bit dated.

I have tried to update a few things where possible. The Chrismatic Snowman in Night of the Long Beards, for example, originally played its music via a tape (remember them?), and I updated this to a disc and inserted a couple of lines making reference to Bluetooth and Wi-Fi. That was easy to do, as was changing the dates in Stars. Crossing the Border was okay because it is set in a timeless place anyway. Ultimately, once the truth is revealed, it really doesn't matter that The Man died in the Falklands War or that the play references The Gulf War and Northern Ireland.

In After School presents rather more of a problem, however. These days, when everyone carries mobile phones, tablets and laptops, the situation in which the teachers find themselves is highly unlikely to arise. In fact, the brief reference to mobiles was not in the original script and was added at a later performance because even then, mobile phones were becoming more widespread. At that time, it was plausible that the younger teachers might have them and the older teachers might not. If anyone were to stage this play now, it would have to be done as – and I hate to use the term about something it feels like I only wrote recently – a period piece. Perhaps a note in the programme would do it, or even, if the set includes a whiteboard, a date clearly written on that. I would say, however, that if an imaginative director wishes to set it in the present day and throw in a couple of extra lines to explain why nobody had any tech with them, I have absolutely no objection. If you do, I would love to know how!

Speaking of which, I don't imagine that the publication of this collection will suddenly result in a huge influx of groups wanting to stage these plays. If you are an amateur group, I understand how times are tough and won't make any royalty charge for you to perform the play. I would expect, though, out of courtesy, that you will contact me so I can give you written permission first and that you agree not to make any changes to the script without asking. I'd also greatly appreciate it if you buy a full set of copies rather than photocopying, so I can eat sometimes. I'd love to be tagged in any publicity you do and see any photos, and please use the TAUK Publishing logo on any publicity. I can send you a background-free version. If you are a professional group, or, say Netflix, or someone like that, it puts a different complexion on things and all copyright laws apply. Either way, if you are interested in performing one of these plays, please email me at the address below, and break a leg!

bobstone189@gmail.com

By Bob Stone

Published by Beaten Track Publishing

Missing Beat (ISBN 978-1786451989)

Beat Surrender (ISBN 978-1786452863)

Perfect Beat (ISBN 978-1786453440)

Out of Season (ISBN 978-1786452474)

The Custodian of Stories (ISBN 978-1786455529)

Faith's Fairy House (ISBN 978-1786454782)

www.beatentrackpublishing.com

Independently Published

A Bushy Tale (ISBN 978-1530960583)

A Bushy Tale: The Brush Off (ISBN 978-1537233789)

Letting the Stars Go (ISBN 978-8750565467)

TAUK Publishing

TAUK Publishing is an established assisted publisher for independent authors in the UK.

With hundreds of titles including novels, non-fiction and children's books, TAUK Publishing is a collaborative-based team providing step-by-step guidance for authors of all genres and formats.

To sign-up to our newsletter or submit an enquiry, visit:
https://taukpublishing.co.uk/contact/

For a one-to-one advice, consider scheduling a Book Clinic:
https://taukpublishing.co.uk/book-clinic/

Connect with us!

Facebook: @TAUKPublishing
Twitter: @TAUKPublishing
Instagram: @TAUKPublishing
Pinterest: @TAUKPublishing

We love to hear from new or established authors wanting support in navigating the world of self-publishing. Visit our website for more details on ways we can help you.

https://taukpublishing.co.uk/

SCAN ME

Printed in Great Britain
by Amazon